A growing list of your author's books
are attached in the back of this book
for your inspection.

Get the
Spirit

Comprehensive Views on Spiritual Freedom

Lloyd E. McIlveen

Order this book online at www.trafford.com
or email orders@trafford.com

Most Trafford titles are also available at major online book retailers.

Print information available on the last page.

ISBN: 978-1-4907-3876-5 (sc)
ISBN: 978-1-4907-3875-8 (e)

Library of Congress Control Number: 2014910230

Trafford rev. 11/18/2016

 www.trafford.com

North America & international
toll-free: 1 888 232 4444 (USA & Canada)
fax: 812 355 4082

A note from your author

The following scripts may be considered a bit dubious and provocative for some readers. In view of that possibility, I highly recommend if you arrive at a point in this book where you are not comfortable and choose to close the book; "do" continue to finish it. You may be surprised to discover how disagreements can turn into more pleasantly relative perceptions of spiritual views we all have in common. Even though I may be a little one sided in my views, I highly respect your views may mean as much to you as mine do to me and "that" right we do have in common. I have always looked at your view. Now you can see what I have to offer. Thank you and "us" for these exchanges.

Preface

The subject of spirit has been around for, indeed, a historically long period of time and will continue flourishing in the hearts and minds of humans for as long as mankind survives.

The proceeding chapters on spirit offer a chance to peek into other perceptions of what the world of spiritual existence and spiritual mysteries may be about. Your author has deeply and ardently attempted to please everyone in the following display of spiritual variations with the knowledge where pleasing everyone is a little unrealistic. That means, of course, the content of these scripts will be somewhat biased toward individual acceptance of responsibility for their lives while developing a more stable form of spiritual awareness and guidance that becomes a supporting comfort in dealing with life's challenges, desires, doubts and curiosities.

The context of the book is described in fairly plain language with a little stretching of the mind in some of the terminology. Each chapter focuses on various and relative aspects of spirit, spiritual, spirituality and belief that accompanys them.

The contents are not primarily directed at converting the reader to be more spiritual or less spiritual. It is primarily directed to be influencial in expanding one's present spiritual perception or outlook for achieving a more stable and secure sense of believing and accepting life as compared to experiencing the worry, stress and feelings of guilt that hinders living an uninhibited life of freedom to think, feel, express and be realistically confident and secure.

There is, in other words, much more to the understanding of spirituality than conventionally professed circles of theology allow people to learn. This is just one of the alternatives explored. It isn't radical. It's wholistically healthy and can only add knowledge and belief of which doesn't take long to make sense for anyone of any state of consciousness whether one is deeply involved in any particular area of spirituality, whether one is in an interim state wondering or probing into or around spirituality or whether one has had no consciously known spiritual background.

These scripts will also serve anyone well who has settled for a stark reality where everything in the universe can be rationalized over, through and by scientific views while comparing views from the theological standpoint. Openmindedness is intelligence.

Your author and many other people spoken to have discovered the subject of spirit difficult to clearly understand and describe. This book deals with the task of helping to understand the nature of spirit a little more creatively.

Your author writes on the subject of spirituality in such a manner that allows one to hear, see, feel, think and generally sense one's inner and surrounding awareness in another perspective that may seem somewhat unconventional. That's for the reader to decipher.

Even though the contents may seem a little odd or even a little controversially annoying at times, it "will" make one think probably enough to start asking more questions. That's what makes us learn more.

Make no bones about it, this is a serious study for the benefit of gaining wider perspective on a subject where everyone is exposed to whether one is involved or interested in the subject or not.

This "is" only one author's views on the subject of spirit. These views have been gathered from religious institutions of all faiths and creeds near and far, from dedicated people who exercise an "art," if you will, of spreading spirit of all natures, the spirit of patriotism, the spirit of sports, the spirit of politics, the spirit of confidence, the spirit of wholistic belief along with the power of spirituality within the self conventionally known as God within and not particularly thought of in a theological manner. This is an updated adaptation and version of spirituality in general.

This text of spirit stretches the old time version of spirit which is ancient religious spirit, the spirit of the dead and the rather dramatic spirit of haunting ghosts which has been reduced way down from a very serious state of fear to more of an entertaining comical spook aspect of spirit.

The spirit elaborated in this book is an attempt to, especially for those who live a rather dull life, "get" the spirit; almost any spirit to feel a little more "alive" about life.

"Getting the spirit" can open new doors for being enthusiastic about that aliveness and then opens even more doors for more insight and helps make life a little, if not more, interesting. Learn about and feel it. It's here.

Contents

Chapter 1

The formation of spirit

The term spirit, in relationship to mankind's soul, is that which cannot be seen, touched, heard, tasted or smelt generally. Unproven claims have been made of having experienced seeing and hearing spiritual images and post death scenes. Let us probe.

Spirit has been known to be the thinking and believing process of the human mind that connects with a source greater than our own intelligence. The most profound connections are those of which exist within the realm of belief. Provable evidence of spirit being tangible doesn't exist since spiritual existence is not comprised of material consistency and only exists in the conscious and subconscious area of the human mind.

Sure, there are computer images of the brain displaying color fluctuations of brain waves etc., but that's only reactions of psychobiological variations, certainly not the invisible "soul" that motivates the thinking process.

The invisible and somewhat indescribable and incomprehensible actuality of spirit has led mankind to "grasp" onto variations of spirit which has also led them to maintain one of two options; to believe or not to believe. Believing in spirit has its benefits of emotional security along with its uncertainties, demands and expectations. Not believing also has benefits of "no" demands or expectations, but one must also accept being completely responsible for the possibility where the spirit of our mind (soul) will stop when we stop. It isn't a matter of what's right. It's a matter of what one chooses to think of and believe. Right and wrong, in the broad sense, exists "only" by virtue of one's opinion or by a majority agreement. Anyone can say, "That's right" or "That's wrong" and where does it go? Usually nowhere when there is little support behind it; mostly opinion. These terms deserve consideration when evaluating choice.

If one is trained or a better word exploited, from a very young age to spiritually believe in an orthodox manner, the ongoing results will be a profound and most of the time unchangeable or unbreakable belief system of mind. Right or wrong has nothing to do with it! Where this condition exists and spiritual belief is firmly formed in the brain, any opposition or views to the contrary will not be accepted or tolerated in so many cases. It's simply referred to as being "set" in the mind.

The power of belief is the strongest "tool" we have for building confidence in motivating our lives regardless of what direction it goes especially when we do the act of convincing ourselves we are "right." Direction also is not a matter of right or wrong. It is "all" a matter of how we were programmed or how we "are" programming at present.

If we had strong and close family ties with spiritual training and majority values, we probably will only believe in that ongoing status quo frame of believing.

"Any" spiritual belief is only as good for confidence, security and accomplishments if it is strong, set and unwavering. Needless to say, there are many different avenues of approach toward attaining that comfort. Generally speaking, there is the somewhat narrow, limited and very strict rules orientated spirituality and there are the open, broad and not so limited views of spirituality. One is justifiably as real as the other. Again, it's a matter of whether one "can" or "will" allow a choice of one or the other. Some people are firmly set and others are not. Some are able to understand their programmed existence within stringent barriers and "choose" to search other avenues. Some are uncomfortable with unlimited possibilities and "choose" to take a firm stand on spiritual views. Some either continue existing without spirituality of any kind as do animals, insects or smaller life and others make decisions to adopt unique and independent sources of spirituality within which are not contingent or dependent on ideals of conventionally established indoctrination.

Spirit is a formation of thoughts, ideas, ideals, views, perceptions, perspectives and beliefs of a living mind. Spirit is of the mind regardless of how the mind functions. It is alive.

Spirit does not exist prior to conception or after death. It is only alive in an individual when that individual is aware of that existence being alive. If it cannot be perceived, it is not real or alive. This contention of perceiving is based on a belief when one has died, perception no longer exists and with that, there is no such thing as the "universe" anymore as far as that individual is concerned. The universe only exists when it is "perceived." A dead person cannot perceive.

Therefore, the formation and utilization of human spirit has existence within. There are unlimited possibilities through spiritual awareness and can be tapped for knowledge, various assistance and programmed guidance within the self.

Science and spiritual research applied to the test may not exist in a compatibly parallel manner, but both are consistant with belief of applying spiritual consciousness for everyday objectivity. Science and spiritual concepts are both similar since they both strive to think, believe and practice their creeds and purposes. They may both be viewed as opposite poles striving and circulating everything on Earth to keep mankind in a growth process of reaching out. However, spirit is generally more inclined to be related with conventional religion, metaphysics, religious science and now the newly extended versions of all of them including the so-called nonbelievers.

Do atheists exist with any form of spirit or spirituality? The term atheist has had connotations of traditionally being antagonistically obnoxious toward a belief of an almighty originator and ruler of the universe. Most of these people agree with one another there is no similar or image and likeness to or of mankind as a God or a "he" or "him" living (as humans think) out in space somewhere or wherever.

The absence of accepting a God as being real does not necessarily mean there is an absence of spirit or spirituality; not at all. All natural spirits are inherent in all humans by virtue of being born and are automatically exercised in everyday life without many people being aware of them. Basic spirituality has a long list of options to either be trained into or choose from and/or develop at will by the self.

Even one who doesn't accept the concept of an almighty can create and develop a spiritual manner of thinking and believing within the self completely separate of civil, traditional, religious or other community influences.

The formation of spirit must not be prejudicially discounted as being bad, wrong or foreboding in any manner. Remember, "all" people believe "their" manner of believing is right, just, fitting and proper. Their spirit is the "way" they believe and that is a result of their developed spirituality from choice or rearing for as long as they choose that privilege.

The formation of spirit began or begins now when one acknowledges there is more in human existence than just a body and a head as smart as one might be. Adopting and nourishing a chosen form of spirituality can enhance one's pleasure in life while creating a more efficient system of security, confidence, impetus and self-esteem. The formation of spirit isn't like a building foundation or a business foundation that needs substantial and required material and energy to function long and effectively. Spirit is only a formation or reformation of gathered information which is either limited or unlimited perception of mind. The formation of a building requires a set foundation and doesn't change. Spirit has flexibility. A formation of a business "requires" flexibility for its function. Spirit, in the newer perceived version, "is" flexible within for managing unlimited pleasures and tasks without inhibiting rules, regulations and expectations. It's all personal within the self when one has chosen it to be and will constantly expand one's consciousness in any direction the individual is influenced with, asked for or enslaved with. So many of us are now fortunate and intelligent enough to exercise our birthrights to search out and develop our "own" manner of spirituality.

Now we are ready to flex our views on spirit without being influenced or "vacuumed" in by sources and methods of which tend to unduly and deceivingly exploit and/or sway one into joining and adhering to institutional dogma which gains spiritual control over one's vulnerable insecurities with methods of fear, fantasy and wishful thinking guidelines and terribly outdated history of rules and regulations. That is a big part of very old time spirit and spirituality. We are now passing through an evolutionary period of time where spirit, spirits, spiritual and spirituality are transforming in their natural aspect as well as in their man-made formation over the millenniums.

Spirit, spirits, spiritual and spirituality all change in formation through the ages of time by human beings regardless of their intellectual ability. This is what these texts are about.

Forming spirit, getting the spirit or believing in spirit somehow infiltrated everyone in different manners: All living beings exercise and live with one type of spirit or another, so there is no reason to suspect or believe some type of spirit is better, not so good, weird or to be prejudiced against. It's interpreted any way one chooses it to be. That makes it fair for all. Enjoy it. It won't bark back. It isn't really spooky.

Chapter 2

The motivation of spirit

Spirit, although not comprised of any material substance, is an exuberantly enthusiastic motivation in itself. What motivates it? The following are statements in question indicating which came first, the alive subject that created spirit or spirit itself that created spiritual aliveness. Read and determine what may be the best answer and compare it to the list after #10.

1. The horse stood quite. Then he decided to run. His spirit arose and became robustly alive. His inclination to run triggered his spirit. Example of best answer: The horse already had spirit. Running just stimulated it.

2. Spirits of ammonia became potent and strong to the nose when alcohol and ammonia were combined. The spirit came alive and woke up the unconscious man.

3. The spirit of politics. The presentation of passing a new law inspired congress to debate it. The spirit was felt by all.

4. The spirit of seventy six. Independence, a high degree of spirit and an overwhelming feeling of pride was gained.

5. The psychic burned insense and told some tales. The spirits were running high and easy to believe. Both the psychic and the client were in a trance (a spiritual sense of feeling).

6. The community spirits were adjoined after the mayor presented the new plan. Much energy was expedited and spirits were high.

7. Spirit of bravery. The soldier made a decision to release his fear and struck the enemy with faithful spirit.

8. The musical group worked and played as one and the spirit was overwhelming. They were spiritually synchronized.

9. Everyone prayed in the church together. The spirit was felt by all in particular because they were all spiritual in their beliefs.

10. Divine spirit is most always connected with an almighty entity which is usually assumed to be outside the human body. Consider these answers:

1. Already answered.

2. The two liquids produced a spirit.

3. Submitting the law for debate started the spirit.

4. The spirit of independence was well engaged much before the actual signing of the declaration.

5. The client brought the spirit in for adjoining.

6. The energy expedited created the spirit.

7. Releasing his fear was exchanged for spirit to charge.

8. The spirit was potential and just needed stimulating.

9. The belief of spirit was first. The feeling of it came next.

10. Divine spirit is potential and experienced when believing it.

Look for what was existing first to determine what motivated spirit so there is no misunderstanding about what spirit is, how it begins, how it unfolds, how it is utilized and how it serves its purpose. That's what these texts are about; understanding much more about spirituality than only what was theologically taught from its bases of historical times. After all, we were all given the opportunity of mind to understand everything changes with time. Everything begins, grows and dies or changes in perception with the advancement, misleading, misunderstood or declination of belief.

There are times when spiritual motivation is a little difficult to maintain in the conscious forefront of the mind due to its rather misty, questionable and abstract sustenance and inforeseeable cognizance that tends to test one's patience as your author may be doing at present.

Spiritual nature isn't boxed, canned or ready to be handed out just because one chooses or expects it to happen. It is a natural response when someone or more propagates reasonable stimulation for something to happen. Nothing from nothing results in nothing which is a pretty lackluster spirit. So, expecting a particular spirit, spirits or other spiritual influence to appear from an uninspired nothing is like expecting the stars and planets to circulate before the universe is even thought of let alone formed.

Motivation for spirit to exist, increase and be of any use, help or perpetrate must be activated by an alive conscious mind. It does not and will not function from unproveable sources of man created divinity of which is only a few thousand years old of human time and already outdated and brittle. The test of time now is, more than ever, having to be constantly reaffirmed of its validity. Without that constant reaffirmation, the assuring emotional support for those outdated beliefs of the ancient past will surely crumble as anything else that requires constant reminders and shoring up. Everything changes just like the whole universe does.

Motivation of spirit is humanity's acceptance of responsibility to initiate workable beliefs within having the same potential and power as catering to or worshipping an unknown, unseen, unhearable, unsmellable, untouchable and unapproachable almighty. This view is only to suggest utilizing intelligence for expanding on available options.

So many of us are looking for what is true, real and fitting. Remaining too set in our ways is not a virtuous spirit of mind. One will not even understand which direction in life to pursue without expanding one's consciousness in different directions. Hoping to be lucky isn't enough in these expanding times. Believing in something "just in case" is hypocritical, manipulative and is an indication of a very insecure state of mind. Any mind "can" transform to a more stable state of mind by observing new or "other" alternatives for possible adaptation or adjustments to newly arising beliefs of universal realities.

We are indeed either #1, subjects of circumstances and influences that establishes dependency on conventional views of spirituality where motivation of it stems from rules, regulations, promises, fear and sheer hope, #2, self-sufficiently and spiritually motivated for allowing a natural spirit of enthusiasm or #3, victims of circumstances of which or who overwhelms, stifles and limits updated spiritual motivation of our future.

Having reason for putting something into action, whether it is for believing, making decisions or for purposes of stimulating is the same as motivating the cause. That means, for instance, a rally for change is only as effective as the reason behind motivational enthusiasm that promotes the rally. This is motivative spirit in action for growing spirituality.

What "is" the spirit? It cannot be seen, touched, smelt, heard or tasted etc. It can be sensed from a short distance and felt by the individuals rallying though. Those are real systems of spirit. Spirit can be thought of, believed and emotionally noticed, but only with reason that supports the notion. Everything has a reason for its existence and spirit is no exception especially when the subject causing spirit is so very loosely utilized and taken for granted as something absolute and almighty. That's wishful thinking only. Absolutes do not exist.

Most of us are trained to believe a certain way at a very young age before we have an opportunity to expose ourselves to various theological and philosophical views of life and death. That type of training usually avoids reasons for and questions why and how things of the ancient past happened. The theology behind it being it is more blessed just to believe and not question the authoritative dogma already established. The reality is the authorities only have a personal opinion concerning many of the innocent questions and they are not permitted to speculate on questions that may expose a contradiction or flaw in the rules for man-made beliefs. That could open possibilities that may "pop" their bubbles of believing. Also, many answers to questions of reality, logic and facts that need proving as compared to only believing are just not available. Believing is necessary for a sound base of thinking, judging, planning and maintaining life's activities and "choosing" a spiritual manner of believing of which enhances its strength for reliability. What else is necessary is to not believe everything we hear or read just because someone or more proclaimed it to be true or because it was written in a book. That means "any" book; this one too!

Motivation in spirituality deserves analyzing and boiling down for broadening one's scope that will add much more meaningful aid for and with human survival in reference to spirit or spirituality.

The major question in this chapter is what does make spirit be spirit or spiritual? We either know what spirit is or we are learning more about it. That's just a matter of gaining more views on it. What we need after that to "get" the spirit is a feeling type of understanding to get it and live broadly with it, not in fear of it.

Getting the spirit is what we are doing now with what we already understand from a creative inspiration, learning from theologians, from family gatherings, from meeting somebody new or from riding a horse etc. How about from sky diving. Spirit exists in us like a breeze that stirs our beliefs and confidence without a feeling of physical change or force of any kind. Those are a few thoughts of how spirit exists for now. Utilizing belief, knowledge and imagination is about as close as we can get without depending on absolute concepts.

Spirit must not be interpreted as a "thing" entering into the body. It's always within. Sometimes it just needs a little encouraging (within that is).

More of this will unfold further as the chapters unfold with more understanding concepts and reasonable practicability.

Chapter 3

What spirit is

Spirit and "the" spirit are two different aspects of spirituality. When we say "the" spirit, we are referring to something specific like the result of mixing alcohol and ammonia or a ghost floating through the haunted house. How about the psychic summons the spirit? All those are specific in existence, not just anywhere in existence.

Spirit, per se, is like an invisible fog hovering around an enthusiastic and harmonious person or group of which cannot be sensed. It is only believed. There is no molecular structure in its existence.

Most circles of spiritual observation have little interest in what spirit "isn't" and have probably invested little time in procuring what spirit "is" other than what, supposedly, "God" or the "book" indicates.

However, further understanding of any type of spirit is a benchmark where anyone can determine how spirit or spirituality fits into their lives. Spirit may be potentially and silently hovering around a situation with a person or people just waiting to happen like a fire waiting to happen. Potentials are nonmaterial and so is spirit. When it's there, though, one knows it even though it may seem difficult to express it or draw a picture of it. When it's there, there is no doubt about it; even with the most profound nonbeliever. It can only be described by the way one feels and becomes excited about it.

Everyone is spiritual in one form or another. Being spiritual is simply a matter of exercising one's natural instincts and let it happen. Even the atheist will say, "I believe I will take a walk." How about, "I believe its going to rain." "I believe my son is a genius." A few thousand other beliefs of similar natures prevail for the same person. Belief is a matter of being confident as mentioned earlier. Confidence is spiritual and their is certainly reason and motivation behind it; all of which is not sensorially perceived, but most certainly believed and not questioned very similar to the unyielding belief in "God" for those who choose that manner of spirituality.

There are many unsure and mixed feelings, ideals, doubts, views and approaches to what most of us perceive as "God" even with extensive training and study on the subject as your author has experienced.

Most conventionally religious people are so very set on going to another "place" after death as though it is so important to live forever where they cling to a concept of spirit as being some kind of a power that transfers them to and in that direction. Even the beliefs of "going" somewhere after death has no logic in it.

Your author doesn't contend it is not true. Your author only says, "I don't know and I thoroughly believe no one else does either; where it's all guesswork or "sheer believing in fantasy" and is a prime example of spirituality functioning in full swing. Sheer believing is spirituality functioning within the self whether it is exteriorly or self-exclusively instigated.

Everything within the self is real and not so questionable. Spirituality within is most favorable for confidence in choosing, understanding and accepting the raw realities of life for broadening purposes and moving forward, like they say.

No assumed spirit beyond or outside the human entity is of any human spirit. It is of man devised conjecture and mythical in nature. The human spirit is only "experienced" within the self. Even though the appearance of a great spirit seemed to exist at a football game, it is still only experienced within each person. The hovering "fog" of spirit existing throughout the crowd had no provable substance that could be termed as anything other than decibel vibrations of applause and maybe some wind. The spirit is the bubbly enthusiasm expressed from each person which may lead one to misconceivably believe the spirit of the crowd was somehow intertwined. The perception of the crowd was strictly emotional and had nothing to do with "a" spirit of the whole crowd.

Don't be fooled, misinformed or become a victim of misconstrued contentions descended from generations of the ancient past to recent times. The following is classic reasoning for not adhering to false spirituality: Praying for the self to make improvements and be more spiritual as time passes is fine, great and necessary. Praying for others has implications of being an invalid approach. Being spiritual sympathizing, empathizing, wishing or hoping to help without even making an appearance is also invalid. It is totally, practically and scientifically illogical for "any" spiritual belief, communication of thought or prayer to travel beyond the surface of the human entity. That only exists in belief and belief doesn't travel. That has been an error in belief for too long of a time.

Consciousness is our thinking process we are aware of. It is within our human psyche. It does not extend beyond the surface of our skull. True, brain waves are detected with the slight penetration through the very surface of the skull's skin by an electroencephalograph machine and records brain waves within, but is not effective in any detection of brain waves passing beyond the skull and travelling through space.

Electricity does exist in the neuropathways of the brain (thinking process) and currents of electricity do travel through the brain. Those currents only sustain enough energy for brain function and that's all!

An electric current requires a direction for it to move, otherwise it will move in a scattered motion like lightening. The electricity of the human mind directs well inside the head, but a person's thoughts are unable to direct the very low electrical energy of thought in any direction outside the realm of the brain partly by the lack of sufficient energy to travel distances and partly by the complete lack of directional control. The idea behind this reality is to not be misled that belief alone can move a stone or even a thought. Everything requires sufficient energy to move it. Believing "God" will change "our" creation of climate change is only wishful and illusive thinking. We caused it. We have to fix it!

The electromagnetic force or pull as it may be, in our our atmosphere, is not a relative factor for assisting in the assumed and wishful belief where direction and destination of the prayer will be attained and completed. The postulation spiritual control will change the course of natural events as in the form of transferring thoughts across the nation through mental telepathy or "God" is just about as far fetched as talking to the man on the moon and expecting an answer. Let's get real so we can get something accomplished. After all, these are modern future times of more reality than ever and dwindling times of antiquated forms of beliefs in fantasy.

If we could send messages out beyond our heads, we wouldn't need telephones or cell phones which are, by the way, energized by more powerful electrical currants than the mind has and are designed to send messages via specific frequency channels. The mind is incapable of exercising such phenomenal feats.

However, all that contentious theorizing is only a humble deduction of your author and not a contention of absolute truth since most circles of the highest intellectual degree agree there is no absolute of anything.

The following is "one" example of spiritual existence: Ray's wife died recently after being together for fifty years. He is getting adjusted to being single and misses his wife heavily. He says her spirit is in the house and he talks to her everyday. Ray is an uncomplicated and very religious person. He believes his wife is in heaven talking to him. He is a very likeable and sensible person and not at all eccentric. Appearances are he wants her back so much, he is wishfully simulating her attendance with his inherent imagination or mental vision.

Most of us understand when someone dies, they do not return. Some of us, though, cannot fully accept the permanency of death for awhile and sometimes longer. This is where and when the misunderstanding and/or stringent prior training plays tricks on us. Ray has been a victim of those self-inflicted tricks, if you will, he allowed to grow within himself over a period of time. He was raised and lived a very Catholic life and never questioned anything pertaining to his religion of which his parents bestowed upon him at a tender age. He had a limited manner of influences in thinking and believing. All symbols, rules and spirits existed only as he was strictly taught and that was his only reality.

Ray's domestic and spiritual chips were down and he was faced with clinging to his profoundly set views on marriage, spirituality and other rules or pass through timely periods of broadening "his" scope in understanding and adjusting to many new views on spirit. He emotionally and spiritually prevailed with his religious faith because that state of consciousness offsetted his grief. Since that was the case, he didn't expose himself to opportunities that would allow him to grow into spirituality of the future which has no limits or strict regulations. Ray was too set in his ways to flex with any changes.

Most people of the world only understand spirituality as pertaining to divinity, deity, holy, almighty or God and because of those limitations, they miss many other possibilities and actualities that can add to their system of believing for more meaningful assurances and confidences which are exempt from flounderous fantasies.

The dark ages and even some of the later and lighter ages were cluttered with suspicion, superstition, mistrust and spirits of hocuspocus natures. Spirit or spirits were mostly deceptive devices for purposes of manipulation. As the centuries passed and Christianity grew, spirit was toned somewhat more to the holy spirit and has maintained that stance clear up to recent times.

Changes always unfold with new ideas and concepts and that is what is currently happening. With these changes, resistance is also present. That is what is also happening and is part of growth progress.

Hysterically, in our view of time, the question of "What is your religion?" has risen so much throughout the centuries. This is changing too. Now there is so much conflict with religious contentions, stances and wars because of them, the question is slowly reforming to "What are your views on spirituality?"

One doesn't have to be old time religious to be spiritual. Spirit is being reconceptualized as it grows with added and deducted views of which are no longer needed or utilized.

Spirituality is certainly a sensitive subject to discuss and deal with and may continue into the future in a similar manner for awhile. Let us always be ready for flexing with growth and change in this area of spirit and spirituality. It "will" add toward a better world of people.

Chapter 4

How belief serves mankind

Everyone has some kind of belief system. They are all different, though, so how can everyone possibly agree on one system of belief? It's almost too much to ask.

Yes, belief and spirit are very closely related. One might term them as being intertwined. Since spirit is a nonmaterial existence and highly dependent on belief of it, alcohol, ammonia etc., holy spirit, the spirit of the community affairs or the spirit of winning wouldn't be known without it. Holy spirit wouldn't have gotten off the ground without persistence in believing. The right mayor wouldn't have attained the position in office without the belief of the people. The runner won the race because of a determined belief that boosted his energy and skill.

Spirit alone does nothing. It only serves mankind when mankind triggers it with some kind of energy, goal and/or belief. They say there is spirit in the air or there is spirit in the church. How about a spirited idea? Well, none of them will be "experienced" by mankind without mankind initiating some effort to experience the psychological energy of the spirit of which has been idly waiting for a little action that stirs it.

When mankind becomes lazy, sick or looses interest, spirit becomes idle or in some cases, nonexistent. One may have noticed that at one time or another. Even when one is waiting for something that is delayed or detained, spirit is also somewhat inactive. One may call it spirit of anxiety.

Animals running on the plain in Africa are full of community spirit. However, that is also an unpleasant, anxious and defensive spirit of running for their lives. They have an ingrained belief that stimulates their spirit to run; for that of surviving!

Spiritual belief isn't just for humans. Every living thing with a mind has a built in enthusiasm for pleasant experiences or defense mechanism responses. Both require a belief that triggers an automatic enthusiasm referred to as spirit. That spirit can be a quiet, inner, and emotional feeling, a stark and panic feeling to move quickly or some kind of rewarding thrill of a lifetime. It's all spirit where one still cannot touch, see, smell, hear or prove in any way, shape or form similar to an almighty and divine entity one may imagine.

How does belief "serve" mankind? Actually, mankind serves belief. Nothing from nothing is the sum total of nothing. That's what happens when mankind doesn't nourish a belief system. Spirit doesn't get underway without an enthusiasm of belief and belief doesn't get started without initiating it with action; which is to say, "Get off the couch and believe in something that sparks enthusiasm which in turn creates an automatic spirit!" Even though it cannot be detected by the usual senses, it "is," as mentioned, psychologically felt. Writing or drawing a picture of that feeling of spirit may be a very taxing effort even with genius mentality, but it's there.

When the battle of the buldge was in full swing in world War II, the going was excruciatingly rough and painful with staggering casualties. The spirit of the Allied forces was incomparably supportive in defeating the Nazis. The spirit they created through their solid belief of winning with efforts extended did indeed support their inevitable victory. There were times when they were low on energy and supplies where their spirit compensated for weaknesses. Blind to it as they were, they knew it was there. They believed in themselves, their cause and their spirit. They didn't take time to evaluate the verbal terminology of spirit, but they knew it was there. Who thinks of the word God and/or spirit when they're fighting for their lives and country? The spirit is always there when meaningful effort supported by belief is firmly and quietly engaged. That's the kind of moral, ethical, physical and emotional support that can always be depended on regardless of reared or reformed creed. That's the belief of the individual accepting responsibility, applying it and exercising confidence to follow through knowing the spirit is increasing with more of the same beliefs and successes.

The spirit of any living being is not intellectual. It is not planned and it is not expected. Therefore, it cannot be utilized in a manipulating manner to get or be something. Belief can. The service of belief in mankind or any other living being is an enthusiasm and confidence of one or a group of any size that tends to perpetuate upon the boldness of the activity.

Belief perpetuates belief. The power of belief, regardless of what it's in, is the strongest power within the human psyche. However, that power also has potentially serious side effects. If a person is trained or chooses to nourish a violently programmed way of life, for instance, the odds are against that person living a peaceful life and probably won't attain it. Why?

Exercising the power of belief within for purposes of improving the self doesn't adversely affect anyone else. Exercising belief to supercede and reign in control over insurmountable odds is unreasonable and unrealistic. A mouse wouldn't attack an elephant or even a rat.

The confidence of belief certainly won't help to stop a speeding locomotive or assist in leaping over a building, but "will" perform unbelievable tasks within the self or will be influencial in contributing toward actions and reactions of mass hypnosis.

Speaking of hypnosis, the best responses in the application of hypnosis or self-hypnosis is when the subject of the hypnotist is willing and/or confident enough to submit his trust and as much as surrender his defense mechanisms to the hypnotist. That's where belief serves the subject. The subject is constantly aware of what the hypnotist is saying. The best subject and results happen when all fear rests and believing what the hypnotist is suggesting is as safe as it is heard. Belief is serving well in this case and can be typical in areas of spirituality.

Training in self-hypnosis is also available for the individual to develop self-confidence, self-esteem and nourish a more effective manner of believing within for more effective mind programming of one's choice.

Hypnosis and spiritual belief are relative and bear no reason to believe they exist as anxiety of fear. The exception being the questionable use of hypnosis connected with drugs administered by anyone other than a qualified and legally certified doctor for this specific purpose. Always use wise discretion when making decisions to add or change anything within the mind or body.

We humans have unlimited access to spiritual belief. Spiritual believing isn't specifically a theologically trained mind by theologically trained representatives of any divine faith. Spirit is naturally ingrained in our mind and body while it is alive although religious belief also states it is in the soul when the body expires.

Since spirit has been inherent in all of us at birth as part of our basic makeup and we have a birthright to manage it the way we either let it be the way we choose it to be or the way we let ourselves be directed. That means we can let it remain statically inactive and serve us with basic and everyday needs such as maintaining a mediocrally stable mind, it can mean we can be influenced by parents or teachers of various conviction or it can mean an independently nourished and developed manner of spirit chosen by the self.

However spiritual belief exists, there is no escaping it as a natural function of mind the same as the feeling of being alive. It is influencial in guiding us.

Chapter 5

The progress of spiritual awareness

A few thousand years ago before and during early biblical time, mankind was unkind toward one another. Even in those days, mass populations were growing. "Evil" spirit lurked among men and they encroached on others wherever the opportunity arose. Good people were robbing and killing and ruthless people were worse. Something had to change. Rules during those early times of mankind had no direction for following or abiding by. Grab what you can when you can was the opposition to conformance. Killing was rampant because community philosophy and spiritual cognizance was lacking. War lords and conquerors were vicious and the people followed suit. This did, of course, vary from place to place.

The people had enough intelligence to be promiscuous, procreative, lay mud bricks, gather slaves and dominate, but when it came to the brotherhood of mankind, they were lacking reason for mutual serenity. They weren't yet civilized from their awkward and timely beginning.

The evolutionary periods of time left evidence that indicated the people needed something more to grasp onto for emotional assurance and security. Slowly, but steadily, the ones who weren't being abusive searched for something bigger and more creatively influencial. They weren't happy or satisfied with just themselves and the status quo of no inspiring future to look forward to. They were becoming desperate for something with meaningful value to become a part of. They surmised, projected with images and insightfully began forming various belief systems of mind. Somehow, they knew it would be something bigger than they could imagine and indeed it was.

Anything dealing with spirit, security and mind function comes together in bits and parts, if you will, over long periods of time. This forming belief system dates back several millenniums after tribes from far lands apart begat their community consciousness of what they believed possessed power over them. Paths and roads of travel brought them together for pooling their spiritual creations and discoveries. This wasn't the "beginning" of a dire need to expand consciousness for believing in a universal entity; not yet. The different tribes and clans each had a different title for their manner of belief.

The tribes and clans clashed with their different views on spiritual control and guidance. They all accepted title of this newly acquired spiritual power that required years of language variation of sound and finally resolved in a simple sound representing the most powerful belief of all time; God. That was the beginning of attempts to universalize spiritual and almighty consciousness. The word God, supposedly, originated from the word good. Prior to that time, the title of God was Elohim (Hebrew) from the old testament in the Bible which wasn't as spiritually widespread.

The spiritual source of God spread throughout growing communities as a source of power to believe in which would guide, protect and depend on for assurance and emotional strength. "God" became known as an unseen "spiritual" entity that existed in belief only. God was also referred to as "He" or "Him" and thought by many as they still do to be a man of some nature in charge of the beginning, the interim and all the future of which the people yearned to be a part of.

Mankind did have the intelligence to rationalize, conjure, formulate, believe and justify it all for believing what many have constantly and unwavingly contented to be true. However, they haven't yet accepted the fact they have always lacked the "ability" and/or willingness to understand the intrinsic and spiritual significance of the old Gods and the new "one" God other than praying, worshipping or adhering to antiquated and misleading stories from humans seeking glory, fame and rewards for their "blessed" discoveries.

Spirit, in the religious sense, has been known by most people to be materially and communicatively undetectable, but believed especially when they thought and chose to believe they would be protected and receive the requests they prayed for including living, somehow, forever in a place where God's kingdom existed even though they had no knowledge of its existence whatsoever.

Oh yes, spiritual awareness grew alright. Whenever anyone wanted something, they exercised their spirituality in the newly adapted religious sense. When they didn't receive what they wanted or asked for, their faith waivered and previous traditions of anger and hostility resumed.

Time passed and as usually what happens with any new venture, idea or belief, the power of belief stumbled, was chastised and faltered over the years, but finally gained enough support from insecure, righteous, peace loving and glory minded people to create covenantal and peaceful existence between them so as to prevent defeating their purposes of spreading spirituality. This was the testing time of dealing with spiritual interpretation among the members of mankind and their newly established discovery.

Since the time of early religious coalitions and alliances for calming desperation and hostility plus satisfying needs of current and future security even to this day, mankind has been passing through endless transitional periods of questioning what spirit "is." All we "really" know is it doesn't go away. Powerful? It's only as powerful as it is believed.

The term "God" is taken for granted usually as being incontestable, undefeatable, unpredictable, unnoticeable, uncontrollable, not always dependable, indispensable, unremovable along with a few unchangeables while being omnipotent, believed in, worshipped, adored, dependable, loving, protective, guiding, conditionally accepting and also more of these author contrived descriptions of spiritual values that can possibly be helpful if one cares to evaluate for the purpose of understanding something, so far, as only spiritual. All the historical and recent books, ascended tales and very energetically expressed and directed lectures on the subject of "God" do not unequivocally convince anyone or prove the "actual" existence of any form of "God" because "God" has never been described by "God" in any understandable or majority agreed upon manner. The interpretation of "God" has only been described by the limited, very stimulating and spiritual efforts of mankind. That isn't enough to vulnerably place a life influencing belief in anyone who already exists within the human system of mind and body. "God" needs to make an appearance of which we can all understand. "Then" maybe we can "really" believe, but not until then.

After all, belief per se doesn't move mountains. Molecular forces and maybe the existence of what we refer to as "God" can or does move mountains, but we only posses the ability to pray for, believe and move whatever is within our own selves, certainly not any more than that. That God within, as it can be believed, is just as effective and maybe even much more, depending on the individual applying the belief, in acquiring what is needed or wanted within the self.

Misconception of what is spiritual and what may be behind it is also running wildly rampant. Spiritual cognizance and understanding "is" progressing and it is our duty to embrace it in such a manner where "we" can knowingly and understandingly live with it where "we" have self-control with and around it.

We were born with an ability to control ourselves as we grow and mature. Some things we are inhibited with and others we accel in. These are the opportunities, limitations and pressures we deal with through life. Our control over them is the manner in which we spiritually allow or progressively develop our immediate needs or longer term choices of believing.

Spirit, spiritual and spirituality are so very closely related. That understanding allows further knowledge of what spirit is. Then is when it can become a little clearer.

Chapter 6

The progress of mankind's mind

The mind cannot be touched, heard, seen, smelt, tasted or felt similar to that previously described spirit. That contention indicates the mind must also be one of a spiritual nature since it is so closely and indisputably related.

If "God" is of a spiritual nature and unprovable of being anything else, then we may reasonably assume the human mind, being spiritual and possessing powers of control over our bodies and endless projects, activities and maintenances on this earth, is as intellectually capable as "any" other spiritual source.

Spiritual belief can be rationalized as a belief assistance for humans that "we" are the creative promoters, developers and maintainers of all in our environment with "no" other intelligence to rationalize why or how we, the animals, the insects etc., the earth and all in space, came into existence. If that is belief assistance, then what is primary belief? Where a more powerful control of consciousness has been chosen, the number one belief is the same spiritual belief in God. The term God can be used or not. The spirit is within, not somewhere else outside the body or in space. It is of the human mind.

No one can utilize self-confidence and power within when choosing to depend on another source of universal influence such as an almighty ruler. One must choose that almighty figure of spirit to be supposedly guided by or choose individual power within to guide oneself. The term God is also used as God within. Combining the two or choosing the middle ground defeats the purpose of believing in either of them.

Since most appearances indicate we are only intelligent enough to believe and not prove a divine entity, there is enough to believe we have very little intelligence to understand what existed prior to the beginning of mankind and all the universes anywhere let alone what was prior to those before or what was prior to those before those etc., etc.

Now, if we can all agree to the prognosis of the far fetched projection in that last paragraph, we may begin to gain more perception on the down to earth progress achieved by the human species of living beings in the past unknown millenniums of mankind for determining the value and acceleration of their progress. Obviously, there has been some observation and recording of mankind's mental, emotional, conscious and subconscious abilities of approach and application, but records containing clear evaluations of their intellectual progress from their two legged beginning to recent centuries has hardly enough sustainable potential even to begin developing smarts for evaluating the psychological dimensions of the universe's borders etc. let alone delving into the actual depths of time, space, matter and dissimilar relativities to and with our common, habitual and idiosyncratical ideas and ideals of which had limited the scope of them all.

Progress of the human mind is different than the progress of civilization especially with the historical documentation of business, buildings, boats and planes etc. which are viewed at random.

The mind is spiritual and cannot be read by anyone or anything. It may be sensed to some degree by virtue of an opinionated evaluation, but that's only a speculation. Speculation is also spiritual being something which is undetectable other than what is said or recorded. Sometimes spirit seems as though it's nothing at all, but that may be considered negative thinking and tend to waver in spiritual avoidance. We don't need that.

The spiritual mind has never been recorded for history's examination; only what the mind said through words, brain waves or xrays. The actual mind is the mystery of spirit. The intellect grows while the mind conjures as fuel for that intellect.

People get educated for progress of gaining a career, playing an instrument or becoming a politician etc. That's good progress which serves their purposes, but does it serve their mind? Ah, that's the question only the minister or the shrink seems to be active and interested in beside the individuals in question of course. The mind, being of spiritual nature, is the undetectable body of action or reaction. That's spirit. It's there for stimulating when the conscious part of the brain decides to act and is there to react in stimulating enthusiasm of the actual act.

The conscious part of the brain is dependent on the progress of growth to make decisions bad or good. That progress must continue to remain healthy and live long. That progress was only registered in the brains of people who passed it down through the families by word of mouth.

The "progress" of conscious minds (the decision makers) is a little vague from several millenniums passed. Records weren't kept on them since they didn't understand the nature of the conscious mind in those eras of time. Only material records of paintings, bones and pottery etc. were naturally preserved from six figure years back for time evaluation. From that period of time forward several millenniums mankind progressed, but was too suspicious, superstitious and ignorant for delving into the spirit of mind let alone the ongoing progress of it until a few centuries B.C. around the time of Plato and Hippocrates when philosophy, psychology and medicine were developing more intelligently and better records were kept. From that period of time forward, the progress of mind including the spiritual aspect became a priority for those who desired a more civilized society of humans.

Mind is spirit and hasn't been commonly, religiously or scientifically measured for growth in time. Value and quality of thinking and feeling are also spiritual and hasn't been measured for timely progress other than an opinion of them. Only the written ideas and thoughts which were scribed or written have displayed signs of timely progress and that began when plates, scrolls, archieves and libraries were invented. One might say all these creative thoughts and ideas of mind were a process of discovery before contentions of them were well established. The maturing advents of contention, debates and arguing led the way for an oncoming surge of intellectual progress of which varied from one nation to another in a fairly long span of time from a few centuries B.C. through the dark ages into the eras of British and Roman Empires. Then, progress of mind became more noticeable and records were seriously formed and preserved for future use.

The subconscious mind is a storehouse of memory absorbed from seeing, hearing, tasting, smelling and any other physical feeling. All of these senses travel through the proper channels into the subconscious area of the brain and store as knowledge and information. This storehouse is the makeup of one's character, beliefs, contentions, abilities, virtues, hostilities, personalities and addictions etc. of which are available and ready to be tapped and utilized for expression of any action by the conscious mind. This can be referred to as spiritual activity.

When a person is born, that person has essential mental and emotional makeup like personality, character, common sense and other basics for survival. As that person grows, those basics change because of being exposed to a steady stream of influences shared, demanded or expected or all of them by relatives, then teachers, then friends and later an influx of new people, influences, circumstances and exposures. Those exposures "feed" new information, knowledge, good or bad, into the subconscious mind for improving and broadening one's mind or for the purpose of exploiting one's mind for specific and/or limited purposes.

The progress of mankind's mind, in general, is more significantly viewed from the standpoint of the individual's progress and not from the progress of the masses. The progress of the masses is mass confusion since they are all so different. Being aware and knowledgeable of many people over a period of time can offer one an average view of whether time has treated the progress of mind very well or whether it has reduced the potential and quality of it. Are we better off or not? That is the classic questions and what does that have to do with spirit since spirit appears as unseen, untouchable, unfeelable, unsmellable or unsensed in any way except by the imagination or acquired belief?

Whether we are better off or not can be viewed in a spiritual aspect of whether we have all progressed in a mutual agreement of spirituality in a compatible manner with one another or not. That seems most important for the harmony of mankind on this planet.

Sure, it helps to understand more about this nonphenominal state of spirit, especially when it's related to the ongoing question of belief, but we might be going unconventionally too far with questions that deal with what we can do about it. Some of these speculative answers may not be practical to relate with in our everyday encounters.

Leaving the rain soak in as it does, we may be better off viewing the progress of mind and spirit of mankind as having learned plenty for now at least in this chapter where the process of mind expansion may be better off just eliminating historic errors from excessively rigid ideals of which, so many times, prevent updated spiritual allowances. Let's bring more people together in peace and harmony in a bipartisan and nonconflicting manner. That way, inner security will prevail and the progress of our spiritual mind will mature with nature as it was speculatively meant to be. In other words, we need to take periodical breaks in pursuing anything as mysteriously conceived as spirit.

Chapter 7

The praying masses

Appearances are such where the majority of the people on Earth believe they are religious. Are they just church goers only concerned about going to heaven? Maybe they want to do what the rest of them are doing "just in case." Could it be they are sincerely interested in becoming better, more loving and caring people? It seems reasonable to speculate all churches have all natures of people even though they all appear to believe and act the same. They spend time singing, praying and cleansing their souls, if you will and afterward get into their cars, move out onto the road and join the dogs eating the dogs cussing and crashing into one another venting their unforgiving natures.

The question is, how many pray for themselves, how many pray for others and how many pray for a cause? When they pray, are they spiritually aware enough to really understand what spirit boils down to or do they just float helplessly along never probing or asking any questions concerning the energy they extend in their lackluster system of belief? Is it like someone or something points them in a direction and gives them a shove and they just keep on going? Maybe some or even many studied extensive theology. That's fine. At least those people are aware of what they have learned. The question now is, are they on the road of broadening forward or are they on the limited road going nowhere? We do have to know we are gaining knowledge to survive and realistically believe.

The mental equipment to survive realistically only goes so far without further intellectual nourishment. The added programming necessary for approaching years better be sufficient for making decisions allowing broad perspective as compared to making decisions limiting, inhibiting and further restricting decisions. We "are" what we are programmed to be, so we had better know the programming well.

The effects of programming can be relative to and/or with praying. Programming is applied to the known self by the self for self-propelling spirituality. Praying is either asking, expecting or demanding something from an assumed spiritual existence which has a name "chosen" by mankind.

The most affective manner of programming is to talk aloud so the ears can hear stating what the self wants to have, give, do or be. The following is an example of spiritual programming:

Simulate a spirit that one can believe in even if it seems unknown. Simulate a belief where it does exist. This isn't much different than relating to a conventional almighty, as the title may be. Many choose programming to spirit within where some refer to as God or whatever symbol or name they choose. Some choose no name. This manner of believing/programming does not extend beyond the body to other places or other people. This is believed as dealing with reality, not spiritual fantasy.

Conventional praying to the conventionally professed version of "God" is effective within the self and many believers agree "God" is a spirit within and not a man, a he or any other symbol of an individual. They also agree spirit is unknown, but does have influencial power within the self where it is real when it is believed. Again, the power of belief is humanity's strongest power within. It is still constantly questionable about it extending beyond the single body or even the body of a thousand people. The power to exercise "any" belief has to be uninhibited and a completely free privilege of anyone's mind in the family of mankind.

When many or even masses of people pray together, they believe they are being influencial in convincing "God" to heal someone or to be victorious in war by virtue of God's help. It "is" true in the eyes of the beholders. What's a belief? Some beliefs are valid and some are not. "Our world is here in space." That's a statement of uncontested acceptance by sane and rational thinkers. "God will come to the rescue" is a statement of contention, belief and hope of which is powerfully positive and optimistic, but remember, the first statement is obvious and doesn't need proving ("Our world is here in space.").

Praying for God's help is not only spiritually asking, wishing, hoping and expecting something, it is believing those prayers will be fulfilled. That's like shooting at a small target. Sometimes it hits and sometimes it misses. The phrase "God does things in strange ways" is a significant reason to question the existence of a perfect power many times thought of as some type of man who invented and maintains the universe. If that entity was so unbelievably powerful and perfect, "He" wouldn't have any problem performing acts of unstrange natures. God within isn't strange.

Why would a person nourish a belief system, of all things, that produced untimely or insufficient results. The negative responses of praying are rarely mentioned and for obvious reasons when related to conventional spirituality (religious).

The tone and tendencies of spiritual belief and practice have always fluctuated and may continue. However, new generations have new ideas and questions of why, what, how and when everything was, is and deserves rational and make sense answers which do not insult their intelligence or demand their support of past, archaic and antiquated consciousness.

Realistically and historically, all belief systems have emerged, grown in different ways with the changes of societies, borderlines, philosophies, cultures and kingdoms which reigned for a time and now are slowly transforming in awkward fashions adhering to the changes and advancing world concepts.

Free and democratic governments do not repress individual choice to believe. Radical and dominant governments restrict and as much as reprimand them for exercising their freedom to believe.

Praying masses are good and necessary when it pertains to peace of mind, helping others, maintaining a civilized society and preventing war. How is that accomplished if praying out beyond the body? One person might not have much effect on those basic virtues. However, groups and/or masses of people praying are not only spending time exercising and believing in something helpful, sharing with others, practicing what they preach and setting good examples they can live by; they are also influencing others to do the same. So what? More people praying together about anything peaceful and good grows and becomes a peaceful and good society. There is power in big numbers and theoretically, when those numbers of praying people become the majority, all becomes well among the people regardless of their expectations. Many times what they were praying for materialized whether they prayed or not, so they continue praying. It keeps them calm and civilized so when they pray for something within, it will have a more positive effect especially when they "really" believe it will happen. Of course, it has to be reasonable praying. Absurd praying isn't being realistic at all. Magical phenomena isn't real.

Praying is conducted and directed in many manners. One doesn't always tell what power or idol is utilized in belief. Many times that is very private and/or not necessary to divulge to others.

I, your author pray too, but not particularly to a man-made version of God. When I pray, I speak aloud and openly to wherever it goes. I believe no one has been given the intelligence to know anything about the creator or creation of everything. That is an inconceivable something and it might not even be that. It's beyond human comprehension. However, being only human, I settle for the growth of belief in myself to solve and resolve matters within and if I am heard by an almighty source, that may be a plus, but so far, my head is not in the clouds.

There are two ways of spiritual praying. One is religious praying via a belief in divine guidance. The other is program praying within the self. They are both spiritual in the sense of them both occurring in the human consciousness. They are both estimated by this author to blend, in time, together and form a spiritual philosophy of a universal nature. This is a must for preventing a situation of spiritual chaos or stagnation with unfolding generations.

Chapter 8

How good and evil fits in with spirit

Generally speaking, religious belief has been known to be good because the belief that God is good. The belief where God is all powerful with assumingly good intentions interwoven appears to be widespread. Are the people (supposedly behind that belief) really that "good" or are they just playing that game of believing "just in case" hoping to go to heaven? There certainly are many signs of contradiction and hypocritical actions among many people with this questionable type of believing.

Mankind, comprised of all different tribes, cultures, nations and clans of many natures, all appear to want peace amongst themselves. How they approach those very nebulous and dispositionistic goals is the bottom line of what determines their virtue in intentions.

Covert manipulation heading toward preemptive domination and the powerful influence of spiritual eminence seem to be the strategy behind conquerors of land and people.

During threat of war between two or more lingering forces, people of all spiritual faith or not, congregate primarily to kill while praying for support from "God." "All" opposing forces will kill one another. That makes them "all" evil. Would "God" support one side and not the other? Western forces believe eastern forces are evil because they kill. Eastern forces believe "God" is giving them credit for killing sinful people and they will be rewarded in heaven. Where does it end? What is right? What is true? How can anyone believe in that or those kind of Gods or that type of spirituality?

Both sides pray for guidance, salvation and other supposed promises before pulling the trigger. That's religious insanity. No wonder young people are casually killing at random. Everyone else in the world seems to justify its legitimacy and publicly advertising it as being an every day way of life.

Obviously, there isn't much conventionally spiritual and general decency, brotherhood recognition or respect flowing through the synapsis and neurons of mind concerning attitudes and actions of these seemingly care less individuals, groups or nations.

There seems to be an overwhelming sense of spirit pushing behind, existing within and apparently destinarially leading from out front with these on sight killings. One must consider the possible reality where spirit has no moral value; only hypothetically insightful, emotionally driven and reactionally trailing enthusiasm of the action engaged.

What does all this theorizing lead too? Glad you asked because if you hadn't, the examples of adverse and hostile actions of community youth coupled with terrorizational hostilities may be too extensive and frustrating as one reads further. It is a growing phenomenon and battle of which cannot be described as bad or good because of allowing for observing the view of the "other" side. Their views are just as important to them as ours are to us.

Spirit, all by itself while being nonmoralistic in nature and not affiliated with any believed almighty, saturates the population of mankind whether or not it is termed good, bad, virtuous or evil similar to the existence and approach of being impartial, nonpartisanal and always available. Both sides of the spiritual spectrum must be examined for personal arrival as to what is valid, fitting or what some people choose to believe as being true.

The spiritual spectrum must "not" be viewed as belonging only to one side especially of what appears to be an opposing, isolated, potentially destructive, alienating or deprivative belief system of mind that only views and directs from a point of self-righteousness and predomination of others.

Probingly speaking and not from a conventionally religious view, spirit is only an unsensible, imaginative reflection of what "God" is believed to be. Adverse, negative or "bad" perception is nonexisting in that observation or feeling. Eastern nations currently accused as being militant, hostile, threatening and terrorizing believe, empower, practice and worship in a similar manner and believe their cause is virtually "good" Those beliefs are benchmarks for their warlike procedures and are only considered as preliminary steps to a gloriously peaceful future either on Earth or in what they term as heaven. Their intentions are of a spiritual nature, not as western nations perceive them as evil or bad.

The preceding views were emanated to project a little more understanding of spiritual perception anywhere other than on a one sided view of which does not particularly represent contentions of your author or publisher.

Based on the contention where humans aren't really bad, but only periodically and/or misconceivably led "off the beaten track," evil is not a part of their human makeup of heritage. Evil is of spiritual makeup per se and therefore nonexisting sustenance and substance. History proves all nonconforming or "evil" leadership and followers have resolved their dominancy and relinquished their control to peaceful purposes as time passes.

The belief in evil spirits date back to ancient times when various forms of superstition dominated easily influenced minds. Little did they know evil spirits were "only" a state of perception and not an actuality. Why, for those who still believe in them, do they seem to exist? Try this: The mind is programmed from birth, as mentioned previously, with domestic necessities, religion, love, hate etc. and later thousands of mind cluttering influences including very misdirected and confusing issues concerning what is good and what is bad. Some societies believe what is good for them is actually bad for other societies. It's all a matter of how one or the society is programmed and continue with it.

Very superstitious or suspicious families or societies pass these beliefs of evil spirits across or down to other segments, generations or decades which highly influences the recipients to actually manifest those beliefs as truth. It's all in programming the mind. Programming can make or allow one to believe in almost anything. The significance of it all is anyone can choose or change their manner of thinking and/or believing.

Spirit, spiritual, spirituality are all relatives and also fit in with all aspects of life from birth to death. One may also "choose," if one feels he or she has the right; to choose believing good spirits or bad spirits continue after death. "I, your author, choose only peace, quiet and nonexistance after death which makes life much more enduring as compared to the hindrance and worry of what may "happen" afterward. Whatever happens will happen anyway regardless of what I believe. Whatever I do while alive has only to do with being alive. Being nothing after death is no different than being nothing before I was born."

Everything in the universe balances. Before and after life, being nothing balances out. Surrounding life around a purely hypothetical existence of something completely unknown in a speculative existence after life does not fit in with the universe's balances of nature. A way of believing is only spiritual and has nothing to do with controlling our hypothetical existence before and after life. Believing in a forever life doesn't fit in nature's balance and is only a hope and wish in a state of fantasy. When the body dies, there is no more spirit. Spirit is only perceived. When one dies, perception comes to a halt and spirit along with it. It isn't good. It isn't bad. It just is what it is. It certainly is nothing new.

Good and evil is like good and bad. "We are the good guys. They are the bad guys" is what they say. Our soldiers are good and their's are bad. That's a crock! All soldiers are decent and family types until they are in position of opposing. By the same token, spirit (not good or bad) exists in all people whether they are on one side of an ideal or the other side. Evil or good spirit, all people think they are right; even with the opposition. That too is only a view.

Chapter 9

Belief origination

How did the senses of belief begin? Many times, people who have been referred to as atheists were thought of or even condemned as not believing in anything; especially anything of which they believed was spiritual or godly in whatever form they professed.

Now we see many centuries and millenniums later by proxy of time and many conceptual changes in belief. People rarely express condemnation or even mention much of anything concerning atheinism. They only refer to them as nonbelievers who don't really say much of anything except they must believe in nothing at all. If there is anything untrue, that is.

It is impossible to believe in nothing. The so-called nonbeliever just doesn't happen to agree with the accuser. The majority believers, most of the time, appear in such a manner to belittle anyone who doesn't conform to their exploited mannerisms and do not seem to exercise any empathy, interest or concern with or about them other than a need to change or condemn them. Seems a good, rational and open discussion may add more lust to expand for both sides instead of allowing further dissension that disallows more perspective "for" that expansion. However, don't bother if one insists on remaking the other. There is a good chance it won't work.

When mankind evolved into a form we presently identify with back in the time of "early man," obviously, they communicated with one another or their societies wouldn't have grown to be what they are now. They would have killed each other off without communicating. By virtue of that contention and maybe consensus, communicating involves reasoning power. Reasoning power requires some type of belief to back it up. Without belief and reasoning power, communicating, as we know it wouldn't have existed and the progress of the human species wouldn't have occurred. We would have remained as animals and maybe not even as smart as monkeys.

Fortunately for what we "believe" the value of human existence is now, we had a pretty good beginning possessing as much intellectual ability as we "did" have.

Most appearances emanate the human belief system originated in one of two places of time. #1. It occurred in what scientific logic and geological research has discovered as the stoneage days which are estimated at one million years ago more or less. #2. It occurred at a time the Bible claims were the beginning of mankind with Adam and Eve of which has no time recording at all. It would behoove everyone to compare a beginning time of anything that has concrete evidence behind it and can be proven without much doubt to a time where evidence is based only on wishing, hope, opinions, belief and ancient scripts of debatable and endlessly questionable content.

Early struggling mankind of the so-called ape or stone age era presented many reasons for mankind to grasp onto and believe for retaining and maintaining their existence in an extremely wild world of hungry animals everywhere. They must have had to form strategies based on what they believed for purposes of survival. The fact millions or more body bones haven't been found from the ancient past gives rise to the possibility masses may have been attacked and consumed by wild animals. The fact they did progressively evolve into and through many eras of future is plenty of indication they nourished and developed belief systems of many natures for mankind's survival to new and recent millenniums.

What did Adam and Eve do to be so accredited with struggling and developing anything? All indications of their so-called beginning were one of beauty, grace and natural luxury. Besides, the only evidence we have of their existence is stated in the book of Genesis (Bible) without clear evidence of their time or residence of unknown thousands of years ago. Those scripts are also extremely exaggerated. The book states individual people lived long lives in named places, but in a completely untraceable time in history. It's like they were suddenly placed on Earth, but there is no evidence when that happened. The theory of evolution makes more sense in logical deduction and proof.

We have considerably more evidence with scientific and geological history from cave wall paintings, human bones, tubes of deep earth and excavated cities in reference to mankind's early belief systems. All those discoveries have disclosed many clues concerning belief origination. Some scrolls are helpful, but all scrolls are open for many interpretations which can be justified by anyone.

Remember, their standards of living were a far cry from ours today. People lied, schemed, cheated, killed, deceived and manipulated without remorse. Civilized religious guidance wasn't yet effective in offsetting that mentality.

So many of the people weren't very considerate of others, utilized their existing beliefs for getting what they wanted and defended themselves in any manner that suited their purpose without feelings of guilt or concerns of going to a heaven. These views of the future had not yet effectively permeated any potential of social and spiritual consciousness of mankind. They were still somewhat wild and not very adaptable in forming philosophical, psychological or religious awareness. Animalistic may fit.

Forming a clear and unconfusing belief system for shaping and maintaining one's life even today, with all the background information and experiences of the past, still requires constant probing and diligence with so many options available in so many areas of thought influence and pressures.

The origination of belief started with the origination of spirit and spirit only exists with the undetectable and unmeasurable belief of it being there. Feeling it is a valid sense, but it cannot be measured or proven to others; only to the self.

Since the origination of spirit and belief are synonymous in nature and only perceived to be a nontransferable feeling within the self, it may stand to reason the origination of spiritual belief has always been when one understands a more comprehensive view of what belief is. That can be considered the beginning and not really a reference of time to the ancient or endless past.

Sometimes we exert effort reaching for something that seems real mystical or somehow out of reach as though, "I'm getting so close, but it's just not close enough" and suddenly or at least eventually, it appears so simple we couldn't believe it.

Well, discovering when belief historically began isn't nearly as important as the significance of how understandably clear it becomes within the self now.

What is really meaningful also is to acquire a clearer understanding of what belief is earlier in life. Your author's book of, "What God is and is not" may help answer many questions and/or gain more perspective into this area of believing.

Our people of planet Earth have dabbled with believing as far back in time as we know and what have we come up with? Realistically, in the overall picture of when and what it has attributed to our well being and compatibility with mankind together, the spirit and cooperation related to and with maintaining a civilized community of peaceful humans has had immense complications in view man himself (very few women) has conjured up so many rules and regulations stemming from insecurity, territorial and disharmonious differences of which has added spiritual haggling over what and how morals and human destiny "should" be and unfold.

The haggling over right, mistakes and wrong is still pending from the very beginning of human consciousness of how to believe. It's nothing really very new. However, with the world's people coming together a little more than ever, belief systems are beginning to merge and scatter. Maybe it's unfortunate, but there are signs where traditional belief systems may prevail for awhile. Humans have always been creatures of habit regardless of the medium of activity. We "are" getting the spirit of it all with each passing day which tells a little more.

Chapter 10

Unfolding spiritual contention

The world's people talk about one God and yet everyone believes in their version of God differently. That's enough to make one cancal it all when it is rationally analyzed.

The question here is why is this unseen dilemma permitted to continue and even worse is whether it "can" be agreed upon and resolved with such wide and partisan views?

Long ago, a man said, "The earth is only as big as you can see." Another man said, "It's bigger than you think." After that, the first man walked as far as he could see and kept on walking. He could see more as he walked and walked until he dropped. The second man walked even further until "he" dropped. The distance was "much" further than both of them thought. Actually, it was endless. They didn't know the earth they walked on was spherical.

What were the two men thinking of when neither guess was valid? They were expressing their ego driven spiritual contentions of being right. Since ego and spirit are insensible and do not affectively register on detection instruments, the state of contention in the conscious mind is often a subject for error. An exception is when majority agreed informational data is gathered to form an undisputed contention where the spirit of guessing is not a factor in the scenario. The two men were guessing with no data. They, like so many other billions of people over time, have exercised the same spirit of contention and gained more knowledge of it through the spiritual state of learning. That state of learning is also insensible and not effectively detectable, but spiritually powerful when exposed to open minded study and the belief where spirit is activated with inspiration, enthusiasm and action.

Sure, we could say the ego drive is behind the spiritual contention to be right. Everyone wants to be right, right? Maybe not too. Some just don't care one way or another. That is, they can be referred to as negative or indifferent in their state of contention. Why contention? Anything one has a stance on and supports is a contention. "I support my candidate." "Sugar is bad for you." "Trains are safer than planes." Also, "I don't care" is a contention. "I don't know" is a contention. How about, "what is right is right" which says, "I'm right." They are all contentions. However, they "are" spiritual because they are insensible thoughts and not subject to detecting; only vocal recording.

Ever since mankind could communicate, physically or vocally, they expressed spiritual contentions. Before they had language, someone pointed in a direction as if to say, "Go that way."

Another person responded to the order and "went" that way from a hand gesture. The strongest person gave the orders in those early days of mankind. Obviously, they weren't aware those nonverbal gestures were spiritual contentions or we as humans would have known a long time ago how to handle and deal with issues concerning spirituality of any kind and all this squabbling about God or no God would have been resolved in our past.

Contentions are statements, attitudes (quietly or aloud) and various other influences, expectations and demands. They all say, "I'm right" or "That's right" etc, "Certainly not," "I'm spiritually right" and yet saying anything about what spirit "is" is a "contention" of spirit because of it's insensibility (cannot be touched etc, etc.).

Throughout the millenniums and centuries, mankind has stood firm with a conviction, idled when not sure and waivered an opinion when unknowledgeable. Those are conditions of spiritual contention. Even the later is a spiritual contention of not knowing. All those contentions exist with action and spiritual response to them.

Spirit doesn't produce, condone, condemn, support or judge. It's just there to be utilized as believing in the wonders, fantasies, glorious opportunities, thrilling and exciting experiences at hand and availability.

People are the determiners of what spiritual contention amounts to, not an almighty that doesn't talk to us and tell us what it's all about. We were supplied with enough intelligence to analyze some of these words, titles, concepts and contention, but apparently not supplied with enough intelligence to analyze and fully understand what an almighty is other than what supposed authoritative representatives of theological circles and the Bible describe. Neither of those are anywhere "near" being sufficiently or broadly supplied with portraying such an inconceivable, uncalculable and mysterious figure of an entity that has been in the spiritual limelight for many millenniums or within the realm of possibility forever. It's all man-made.

Ego driven contentions, inherent from mankinds beginning, have led the way for their progress from the ancient past to our present time. Men (mostly) were compelled to state, argue, debate and/or fight over strategic or even trivial contentions to accomplish objective results or just to prove they were right. Would anyone ever have believed those directions toward accomplishments were of a spiritual nature? Maybe they would if praying was behind them and the results were favorable for the prayers. Praying is another example of contention which is a contention where praying is an effective manner of getting one's way or at least "believing" it.

By now, we are beginning to realize spiritual contention isn't particularly a developed phenomenon over a long period of time. It is part of our psycho-human makeup just as our need to eat or sleep and only increased with the use of more words to describe the contentions. Contention is a human stance to convince and has no prevalence to or with material existence and therefore is of spiritual nature. Words describing contentions are physical pictures and not spiritual. Why? Words are heard, therefore subject to being sensed.

Understanding the progression of anything in this life we feel, see, cherish, love and respect allows us to tap more resources for eliminating many useless fears for the benefit of making more meaningful choices of strategic value.

We will undoubtedly never run short of contentions because of our humanistic manner of progressing through new ages of time plus the fact spiritual aspects and reactions will exist whether they are apparently, cognitively, deceivingly or negatively perceived or not.

The main objective to stay focused on is not the maintenance of unfolding tradition necessarily because reality states everything does change, but to constantly expand our systems of belief in all areas dealing with our spiritual consciousness to learn more about it.

Our spirituality is always with us. It isn't something that was placed upon us initially by a universal entity for us to suffer for with penalties for inadequately adapting to. Not at all! Those are only man-made prognostications conjured up from fear of reprisal from an unknown nature and defeats theological theories of not living with fear. Many of those ancient interpreters of spiritual belief didn't understand what they were preaching. The follow-up was the people didn't either. They just flowed along with it because of their influenced attractions of fear and fantasy.

The preceding statements, as others concerning theological interpretations in these texts, are not stated with intentions of being absolute in contention. That would be counteractive to any possible changing, flexible or contrary views on improved concepts of spirituality and therefore tend to defeat the literary material offered in this book of getting the spirit.

Promotions of absolute belief and related dogma are slowly but surely becoming a thing of the ancient past because of its inflexibility to inevitable change of so many natures of which we are learning. Those who don't will be embarrassingly left by the wayside of rigid causes. Let us all search out further possibilities.

Chapter 11

The conflicts of opposition

Human opposition is also spiritual. It is based on stance of unyielding thought and is insensible to physical or material connection. Spirit is not a subject to be judged as good or bad because there is no describable substance connected with it.

Whenever there is opposition where two forces clash, as in war, the prime objectives are to defend against and/or conquer the other force. The people are usually unaware the fighting isn't "only" a physical and mechanical struggle. It involves a reactionary result of opposition concerning territorial or religious dispute, a resolution of revenge or attempt to acquire dominancy. What they miss in that assumption is as follows:

War is a result of conflicts. Conflicts are a result of opposition and opposition begins with confusion and misunderstanding in expanding societies usually pertaining to ownership of land, natural resources and many times poor communication from incompatible languages and their cultural dispositions and natures.

There are many gathered reasons over a period of time which instigates insufficient and really necessary communication among those who oppose one another. Resolving conflicts causing opposition between individuals are much less spiritually intense as compared to masses of people rallying behind their leaders applying pressure on them to make a move, change something or find an alternate route. Masses forming are spiritually driven.

Masses of people, for instance, around the world have ignored an inevitable financial breakdown that progressively worsened and finally created a landslide of innumerable and intensively complicated problems which provoked a desperate need for governments and our people to finally "face" realities where most of us were living in fantasy believing nothing would change as it caused financial chaos around the world in 2008 and following years.

Opposition to everything seemed to be the order of the day where everyone was arguing with everyone. Everyone wanted only what "they" wanted and didn't have enough desire for what is disciplinally and even sacrificially needed for the financial stability of nations as a whole. This consciousness has inevitably warped itself into a contagion of self-interest motivation and not enough for national or international stability since we are all becoming more dependent on one another as time moves on. There has been a negative spiritual existence hovering over the people.

These notes are exemplary of how one's views of mass spirit exists without judgment of, without prejudice, without any direction of good or bad "and" without any awareness from the people where it has been their own spiritually promulgated actions which have largely contributed to the mentioned financial dilemma "and" spiritual disposition.

The resulting conflicts of opposition are of a spiritual nature since they have been conjured up in the human mind and are not tangible until they become a material battle. Cold wars are conflicts of opposition and therefore are also spiritual.

We are learning anything spiritual is not always heavenly divine, of the dead, grossly ghostly and essentially fragrant or steaming in the lab. They too do have their conflictive oppositions as we have seen in the past.

Where one is talking, walking, driving a car or riding a horse, conflicts of opposition are usually tolerable with some discordant allowance, but in a rickety plane or an off course space vehicle, conflicts of opposition are subdued to a minimum for purposes of preventing a panic and the spirit of action and reaction is steady and calm, but also emotionally stimulated. The tendency under intense pressure is for one or more to either experience the spiritual existence and reactions of remaining spiritually calm as possible, spiritually praying or spiritually believing. Spiritual praying is asking for divine assistance or guidance. Spiritual believing can be a matter of knowing divine guidance is or will prevail or is a matter of utilizing self-confidence and spiritual serenity within.

Divine guidance and self-confidence have been known to conflict and oppose one another, but are relatives in the family of believing. Remember, inner believing has wide spread concepts and views available and are actively in use around the globe.

Conflicts of opposition have existed since mankind could stand and walk. "That's my water hole. Go away." "That's "my" woman." "No, I met her first." "That's "my" cave." "Too bad, I'm bigger than you." All is spiritually calm until one starts a fight. Then, it is assumed the fight is bad spirit setting in. Not true. Spirit doesn't set in from any outside source. It's either there within or it isn't depending on how one acts. It's not good and it's not bad. It just "is" or isn't what it is.

Animals aren't much different with spirit. When the two rams buck each other, their spirits are high, so to speak; not good, not bad, just instinctually there to do what is natural.

Opposition isn't a bad spirit "doing" its thing. It's only a spiritual differentiation in concept until the fight starts. Then, the spirits whip up, but are still nothing to be put in classification of good or bad. That's why evil spirits or good spirits have no merit. They are there for purposes of believing. Spirit and belief are of the same family of knowledge and awareness. They are not to be summoned or discharged like a commodity or an employee. They are just there and are not responsible for anything or anybody. Responsibility is for molecular living beings who are somehow given the intellectual ability to accept or deny responsibility and that is their birthright privilege the same as choosing to walk, talk, kick, love, work, resent, compliment, travel, give, pray, win, lose, hibernate, believe, disbelieve or even die. The exception is we didn't choose to be born.

Rules have only been concretely proven to be devised by mankind and no other source. Now, in the advent of women's rights, social equality and advancement of their positions, women are also making rules. Why are these changes and advancements occurring now and not for thousands of years past?

People have been culturally and religiously habitualized to hang on to their feelings of security until something better comes along. That's human nature and must be understood, respected and maybe even tolerated.

Now, even though opposition to change from the old school mannerisms of belief still lingers, people are becoming more aware than ever of the creaks, cracks, faults, flaws, contradictions and misleading dogma of ancient beliefs and spiritual conceptions.

Now the conflicts of opposition, having gotten underway for many years are presenting a clearer picture from every word of spiritual activity expressed. The more is said from all angles, the more we learn to choose our way from the past.

More education is needed now than ever to handle and compete in world affairs because of everyone going into debt for the past fifty years or so more than ever. Unfortunately, everything has gone too far.

More education "is" needed, but along with it presents opposition and extended views which in turn creates more competition. This is overflowing into and with world business sports, politics and unfortunately again, religious "premotions" and very young people's conflicts with one another such as gang warfare. We have entered into an era where the more people there are, the more intense our opposition becomes. It's all opposition because of the tendencies to compete in any way shape or form. Where is it all going as the question is asked more than ever?

This author opposes the use of hostility for solving local and world problems with the use of logical, fair, spirituality within and moral philosophy supported by adapting with the changes of time. Nourishing all people with that consciousness is a spiritual endeavor.

Chapter 12

The changes of spirituality

When mankind matured around the time they were full sized, humans probably had little ability to communicate with language as we know it today and spirituality is estimated to have been unknown. A rational guess is all we have at present.

Spirituality is a linguistical byproduct of spirit. What little they did have for communicating didn't include concepts and meaning as we understand them today. We know a "lot" more today about spirit or spirits, but look how long that took. If they knew "anything" at all about spirit in the beginning, the progression of change and additional knowledge over many millenniums concerning spirit would have ascended through history much more effectively than it has and there would be no questions about it now. World leaders and clans kept it subdued with fear tactics and unbreakable habits.

Yes, there are still many unanswered questions concerning spirit and spirituality. The archaically ingrained beliefs of spirit, as mentioned, are still limited to divine consciousness guidance of one God. However, the Bible does mention how divine spirit exists within and yet so many people practice the belief that God is in a space or time of heaven and/or everywhere else and travels a lot too.

Your author and many other people spoken to have discovered the subject of spirit difficult to clearly understand without extensive study similar to what we are doing in these scripts. It is typical for spirit to be believed as the Holy Spirit because that's what most people are "trained" to believe. All living beings are subjective to become products of their training, especially when influenced by family, close friends, employers or biased schools and institutions preying on depressed individuals and nations to say nothing of neighborhood residents etc.

We can only speculate how mankind's spiritual actions and reactions were perceived when they began feeling them since there is very little evidence of their perception from recorded history or scientific research. Religious authorities can only quote from the Bible and it doesn't state dates that far back. Science claims reasonable evidence of man's existence from 40,000 to 100,000 years and of course the theoretical stance man evolved from as far back as the prestone ages of a million years more or less.

The burials of several thousand years ago, which is prior to the ancient Babalonians and Egyptians, were uncovered by geologists and treasure seekers of more recent times. Enough evidence for evaluating their life style has indicated the buriers treated their dead respectfully enough where they were detectable many thousands of years later. This is a sign of spiritual values of which many of the hierarchical and monarchal type kingdoms were built on especially in those areas of the Middle East where different "Gods" in material form were idolized.

Spiritual believing changed enormously in those years and centuries of many Gods to fewer Gods when new governments and spiritual philosophy exasperated and confused the people of all ranks. The symbolic statues or sculptured heads representing their Gods deteriorated in spiritual value as divine awareness matured and the people's views of higher power was reduced eventually from different Gods to one over many centuries of time.

The condensing process from Gods to one God was a time consuming struggle to consolidate their beliefs of spiritual "power" similar to present problems of consolidating conventional religious "churches" of which is now an extremely slow process. Each one clings to their "own" manner of believing.

Spiritual development is more susceptible to change and maturity when territorial conquests from czars, plutocrats and totalitarian rules dominate as was over abundantly happening in those horrendous days of conquest and slavery through the Middle East. Later, in the advent of cartographers, business was booming. Every time they turned around, someone was changing the borders and names of the regions (talk about spirits being stimulated).

Masses of people, especially prior to and during the Middle Ages, followed their leaders whether the leaders were religious or heathenistic. The exception was during a revolution. As they followed, so have their beliefs through influences of promised fantasies or penalties; depending on their complaisance.

Down through the ages of time, leadership knowledge gained a need for security and prompted mankind to form and reform spiritual beliefs and adaptations "to" them while rejecting and noncomplying with others. Fear, superstition and totalitarian leadership prevented freedom flowing spirit among the common people in those darker age years. Many systems of worshipping, idolizing or otherwise believing were suspected of sinister and ghostly activity, so the term spirit became corruptly tainted for a few centuries until elementary theology arose, grew and inspired people to be more civilized.

Civilized spirit was needed. The people knew it and allowed themselves to become vulnerable to divine spirit of which they only had hope for. Slowly, divine spirit was adopted in the manner of which they chose to believe and it became a profound way of life believing in something they thought of as omnipotent.

Again, the people slowly began to learn more about what they wanted to believe "in." The community of divine spirit became the spiritual centerpiece for a few dedicated to the new consciousness of believing and it grew into the distant future.

Many stories of divine conception and ascendancies are written in the earlier chapters of the Holy Bible. Some are believable and some are questionable. Others are only speculatively written. This pertains to the entire text of what was referred to as the Big Book prior to the Bible. One must never be passive to the point of believing everything stated in "any" book "anywhere," "any time" lest to be vulnerably deceived.

The progress of spirituality has not only changed throughout time since its inception, but has fluctuated in concept from individual wishing in masses of suspicion and international recognition to almost universal acceptance. It has passed through stages first, of unknown spirit, then of learned spirit limited as it was and evil spirits of which collided with divine spirit in many different manners from the conflicts of belief in them to wars over them.

The accusation or belief in evil spirits are now pretty much limited to the commercialization of them and only technically iterated by certain occult groups, activists and revolution spokespeople in describing opposition to what they believe is better for society or "their" form of society.

The stages of spiritual concepts of which have been developed with time, spiritual contentions which is exercising freedom of belief and institutionally directed beliefs have all unfolded before our eyes in more expansive forms during and after the time of Jesus in what has appearances of giving in, adhering to or resolving with the status quo of conventionally religious beliefs.

When there is freedom to interpret anything, there will also be changes in interpreting spirit of any kind and that is what is happening in this era of time. Spirit accompany's what one will "get," what one won't get, what one will fear and/or what one will continually strive to comprehend and inevitably apprehend for more comfort, flexibility and harmony of living realistically in this life on planet Earth or anywhere else as is mentioned periodically throughout your author's literature on philosophical views pertaining to spirituality, belief, confidence, health for long life, emotional and mental stability, interpersonal compatibility, raising general standards and many more of similar natures.

One or more will never know what is beyond or right beside their present knowledge of spirituality or any other form of believing or living if one doesn't exercise a little or more expanding out from a trained or habitual activity of mind. Opportunities of all dimensions and directions are sitting and waiting to be explored. It "does" seem a little risky, but we can't do it when we are finished with life. All spirit is here for "getting" it.

Chapter 13

The age of choice

Referring to the ancient past once more, the people were much less complicated in their natural environment, social life and little spiritual consciousness they had. Sure, the populations grew and presented challenges that presented more complications. They were faced with having to make more decisions of which were only stepping stones of learning how to survive in a pretty rough age of time, let alone worrying about what will or can happen in the future.

This chapter title, "The age of choice" started at a very young and ancient time. Little did they know they were, like many people might say, placed into a position of having to pioneer human life for a future of many millenniums ahead in time.

The age of choice is also an evolutionary process which spans from the beginning of mankind to now "and" into the future. It doesn't really leave much content of thought, contention or material to write about other than all the combined ages of man's progress occurring as a result of choices made beside natural disasters. It is commonplace and not totally applicable to or with this chapter.

The significance of choice through the progressive ages of time deserves more recognition, appreciation and praise. Recent centuries of time has brought more progress of choices around the world do to the exploding international population. There again, all the ages to the present time have attributes to the privilege and alternatives of choice. That privilege is being promulgated through the systems of psychology, philosophy, family, schools, churches and literature reaching these places for the purpose of broadening one's scope of perception and approach.

I, your author have attended seminars, groups and classes for the purpose of improving my ability to effectively communicate with people of all distinctions for sharing viewpoints of wider perspective. Sometimes this requires making choices to "bend" and even change some of my ways of thinking and believing. I learned to access my acquired personal assets and developed abilities to choose making decisions which "do" represent me while blending with others for the purpose of creating a more compatible scene of relating. While interviewing many people, I have discovered so many of them responded in such a manner that indicated their hesitancy, unawareness, inflexibility and even as much as unwillingness to make choices in particular when it pertained to something they weren't or even were accustomed to doing. This is classic and habitual inflexibility and fairly normal among the masses of people.

People at the dance, in school and at restaurants etc. habitually sit in the same seats---if they can get them. People won't approach strangers, not so much because they are afraid "of" them as much as their restricting habits that prevent them from the uninhibited approach plus the habitual fear of rejection. The only choice that seems to be constant is the choice to be habitually negative. Some may call it "reserved." That's a consciousness justification for, "I can't break my habits and I have limited myself to only a few choices." Even pertaining to smoking, for instance, the justification for that hazardous habit is, "It's something I like to do." If the addiction of habit wasn't so prevalent, the "something" wouldn't be liked so much and could be avoided or "dumped."

Since there is so much more of everything available now, we really ought to have more flexibility to exercise more options (choices.). We are in an age of at least knowing we can exercise them more than ever before. All we need to do is exercise other potentials in our consciousness which some call our brainpower. That ability is also a quiet and insensible spirit. Stimulating it with new orders from headquarters (our brain) will activate the spirit of enthusiasm and make detrimental habits easier to break or at least regulate better.

Gaining more conscious power to make more and better choices means "breaking" through established patterns of habits. Sure, we habit formers feel comfortable doing the same things over and over. Some of them are okay and some aren't. So many of us hesitate because of the possibility it may get worse making decisions to change so the tendency is to stay the course.

The getting worse aspect of it is an erroneous suggestion or belief based on sheer fear. The opposite course is to plan a rational strategy while bypassing fear. This fits well within the age of change we are in more than ever regardless of our set or hesitative habits. They "can" be broken for a more rewarding psyche and spirit of mind.

Spiritual belief is the most powerful self or divine influence we possess within. The firm, but flexible practice of spiritual belief builds foundational requisites for success and success is a result of choosing the direction that works the best for a particular individual.

Building that foundation for success requires acquired knowledge from various chosen sources and the appropriately chosen subject, people or material (maybe all) for the success desired. Without discretionary choice, success is "at risk" with less favorable odds.

One must not play a game of, "I'll try this spiritual thing out and see if it works." That's playing a game with the influences and forces of nature which includes tinkering with divine guidance or playacting with intent to manipulate. The only effectively workable choices are the choices backed by sincere and dedicated belief in those choices, so they better not be haphazard or self-defeating in nature.

The power and freedom to make choices has no limits unless one believes they do. The power of belief serves anyone with any belief. It all depends on the intensity of the belief. Good or bad is only what is contextually contended, has no "absolute" value and is biased opinion which sometimes has contemptuous overtones of righteousness as though "I'm right and you are wrong!" Morally speaking, everything in the universe is "bad" because it devours everything entering into it over a period of time similar to what is happening on Earth with crime, deception, greed, war, mass extermination, natural disasters and threat of all living being extinction. Clusters of stars colliding just happen to be chaos on a slightly larger scale. Compare the two and see how puny we really are, especially when we believe we are so important we have to live, somehow, forever without knowing anything about it whatsoever.

If one's scope of mind and perspective is broadened enough to further understand how one condemns something or someone as being bad or wrong, that person may realize everything and everyone are just as the universe is; not good or bad; just is. Another way is only in individual perception that, "I oppose the stance where the universe is indifferent and judge the universe and everything in it the way I choose."

True, that "is" a choice and that individual is also saying, "I know better where that view of the universe and my perception doesn't accept or acknowledge the theory of the universe and everything in it as bad because of it annihilating and devouring." Continuing with this person's contention; "Furthermore, I believe everything in the universe is God's garden and all life's struggles, threats, fears, stresses and death are planned and meant to be as they are without my questioning "Him." Therefore, only good prevails because God represents forgiveness of everything including the devouring universe and the crime, deception and war etc., etc.

The two views, whether real or believed, were presented in this chapter for exercising one's choice just to analyze, make changes or remain the same. Are there more? Those may be choices too. The privilege, birthright and power of choice must be honored and remain open for everyone to exercise those rights freely and uninhibitedly for as long as mankind exists.

Chapter 14

Dealing with fear

What stimulates human motivation? Is it fear, hunger for food, love, sex, security, spiritual understanding and acceptance or is it all of those?

So many down and practically out people of the world obviously experience more needs to survive. Without food, they won't exist long enough to be concerned about surviving. Sex is a stimulant and they are not lacking in that area with evidence of their population expansion. Love, in any form, is spiritually needed to compensate for the lack of anything secure and fear lingers constantly. Without those stimulants or community help, the underdogs of society would be grossly discouraged and probably slip into oblivious termination. Fear sometimes feeds on fear and eats up all stimulation striving.

People who have steady and good paying jobs or aspiring careers exist in medium security positions where the bills are paid and many family, friends and other community activities are enjoyed through enough stimulating and/or meaningfully developed or supplied attributes of which sustain their social and emotional satisfaction for a length of time.

The middle class fears are low. There is plenty of food. Family life usually presents adequate love, sex and other securities. Religious understanding in this class of people is only as effective in dealing with fear of punishment and future security as they are either "trained" to believe or as they extend perception, perspective and knowledge. That means to search aside and beyond for extended and unlimited views on spirituality "other" than the usual and conventional fear oriented contentions.

The belief or maintenance of one's fears are only as potent as one has acquired them inherently if one had no other influence. Going a little further, since no one is "that" pure and uncontaminated, other influence from birth forward includes that of the assisting people at birth, the parents, relatives, onlookers, baby sitters, housing, weather, parental compatibility, neighbors, teachers, other students, exposure to love or lack of it, exposure to hostility, exposure to stringent rules or to none. Those only pertain to the rearing years of life of which are said to be the most important years of forming one's confidences, beliefs, fears and one's abilities for performing and adapting to the existing and future situations of all natures. Wow, what surprises may be in store for all those people born into a world of acquired fears.

Sometimes it seems fear runs the show of everything. So many cases reveal it only "seems" like one is afraid because of the previous mind programming or other influences from birth and/or further emotional influences one was "vacuumed" into, if you will.

Dealing with anything pertaining to fear is a very sensitive and difficult area of presenting, contending and receiving data for improvement or change. Having said that presents reason for the reader to feel anxious and resist moving further in overcoming fear just because of the suggestion of it being difficult. Even that last sentence could make it worse. That one too!

The old adage of "success breeds on success" sure does apply so much of the time. Failure, by the same token, breeds on failure too. That point is emanated to illustrate the power of suggestion and the guiding use of words for clear and descriptive terminology as compared to words which only influence's one's emotional consciousness. A classic example is how political candidates running for office are quite articulate with words in "twisting" statements around which were made by the competing party. There are "always" opportunities to "everything" which must be allowed, listened to and tolerated for creative relating.

Reading between the lines, as it's said so many times, must be developed to discern the difference between words of manipulation and words of clear and sincerely described portrayals.

One aspect of professional or con manipulation supporting their success is utilizing the knowledge where the unsuspecting victim many times won't be aware of is making statements which work on people's fear and their easily influenced motivation. Once they have convinced the people to be afraid, they become easier to influence in changing their objectives. One thing leads to another and the perpetrator wins.

Only a manipulator can recognize another one, generally speaking. Most people specialize in what they do and don't identify with these unfair practices and become victims of them as well as anyone else practicing similar methods; deceivers or not.

Eliminating excess fears that hinder our everyday lives is helpful, but some fears must be retained where we are exposed to more as in the city where unscrupulous characters linger. When a sheep walks up to Little Red Riding hood, now she can quickly escape. She knows it's the wolf since sheep don't walk up to little girls. Purity is fine, but lessons must be learned.

Fear is also a spiritual existence of which we have allowed ourselves to believe is an emotional anticipation of danger and yet it is the same phenomenon as spirit which is an insensible hypotheses. It becomes a message from the brain that "affects" the nervous system, but the fear per se is only spiritual and has no molecular connection to anything. One might say fear does not exist. Only the instinctual belief of it does.

We were born with certain inherently supplied guidelines of information to survive stored in the subconscious area of our mind (brain) that includes a support/defense mechanism called fear. That fear will remain the same in neuron form the rest of one's life until the psychological shape and disposition is rearranged. Then we can perform wonders within.

Remember, the neurons in the brain are thinking cells. Conscious programming of those neuron cells reshapes those cells "by" themselves. Making a decision to change the neuron cells by reprogramming allows one to reduce, change or add to increasing the disposition of the brain cells therefore altering the belief of fear. That's only part of the power of mind and belief. Read your author's book entitled, "Understanding The Science Of Creative Mind." It will help in discovering, developing and practicing a psychological powerhouse within to add and/or make changes within for the benefit of gaining more self-confidence and self-esteem etc.

Fear is a necessary human asset for reasons of protection, survival and respect. So, even though we could eliminate all fear, it's better to maintain a certain amount for those stated reasons. Let's not get carried away with eliminating all of the fears, let's just eliminate the anxieties which seem to lead the way of those fears. Let's develope a better sense of confidence in judging what our fears amount to and use our fears to protect ourselves so we can move forward.

The doctor says, "Providing a cure for a problem is one thing, but keeping the patient alive is more important at the moment." All seemingly adverse conceptions and conditions also have there opportunities if observed. Making decisions must be guided by best judgment, not by misleading anxiety.

Dealing with fear is a matter of getting the spirit. When spirit, spiritual or spirituality is better understood as a human function and not primarily a connection of some kind with a leader or ruler of the universe, the practical and rational use of the word fear will allow one to make better and calmer decisions when exposed to threatening situations.

A threatening situation as being held up by a gunman is accompanied by a bit of fear or more and must be delt with in a reduced anxious state for best results. Understanding the spirit within helps remain calm.

Worry is also a spiritual function and being a spiritual function within the self, that energy burned in worry can be rearranged into another less intense state of mind as one remembers fear, spirit and joy are relative in consciousness.

Chapter 15

An epochal evolution
(a new and important time)

History has shown us spirit, spirits and spirituality has had their variations of belief and how to respond to them or not. Some religious circles believe it's all part of preplanned episodes of life on planet Earth and other more philosophical groups view it all as just another evolutionary period of Earth's billions of years of existence. Who's right? They're both right. Just ask them.

The one who has written this book has the privilege to be slightly biased in approach some ways and a little more in other ways, but always with attempts to display something new or different from the old schools of thought. They "may" occasionally blend in with current variations of spirit for establishing and maintaining at least somewhat of a compatible relationship with the readers. Bringing the passives and the aggressives, the easts, the wests, the old and the new together for building a web of spiritual compatibility where various belief systems can exchange ideas and beliefs instead of lambasting and bullets seems like more of a mutual interest than putting each other down with forces and fears.

We are all at the crossroads of time for allowing religious deception and turmoil to guide our freedom of spiritual practice of which has had too many variations of belief especially with the so-called divine influence. It's time for all of us to blend with spiritual harmony. If the people of the world subscribe to the theory (or belief) that God is running the show of life on this planet while all appears to be headed for chaos, then earthlings have nothing good to look forward to; only chaos till the end and the theory (or belief) of God or good has no more meaningful validity.

An alternative to unnecessary chaos of life is for everyone to pool the redevelopment of spiritual cognition around the world where philosophical, scientific, metaphysical "and" divine guidance merge and not explode, but condense intelligently for the benefit of everyone. The time is approaching for us all in accepting responsibility for our actions instead of believing we can get help from an existence that doesn't realistically communicate with us and has led us to believe mankind only has exaggerated a divine belief handed down through the ages. There has "never" been any real evidence of "any" God expecting humans to spend time worshipping and supposedly loving what appears to be a self-centered almighty figure of completely unknown origin, existence or substance. Once again, it's man-made.

Try the following on for size: If we were, supposedly, made in the image and likeness of

God, then we would look like and have all the basics of God including the ability to live forever like God supposedly has, but we don't. Everything in the universe dies. Why doesn't God? The only answer to that scenario and question is a guess of which humans have been doing for a long time. If this theory (or belief) doesn't seem acceptable, reasonable or understandable, then again, read your author's "What God Is And Is Not." It explains much more than what is here about old and new views, theories and guidance pertaining to the ingratiating concept of extenuating beliefs in God specifically and in general. There are too many contradictions concerning the existence of the conventional view of God. We must sort them out.

These crossroads of time bring vast knowledge to the forefront of merging communities and nations. Sure, they are all looking for either help or control over the other. Nations in the process are learning, more than ever, to internationally exchange with one another while governments are covertly jockeying for opportune positions of manipulative exchanges. Some are with their hands out. Some are quiet about it and others are openly hostile in attempting to get their way which only supports "their cause."

Regardless of the unseen and obvious intentions of national preditors or opportunists, people of all nations possess inherent spiritual abilities, skills and hordes of assets. Some Middle East nations advocate religious control over government so they can eliminate opposition making it easier to take over other communities and nations by illegally exploiting stolen children to spread their indoctrination around the world slowly, but surely. Some TV documentaries have indicated their efforts may be working okay.

The irony of this scenario is we are talking about, supposedly, religious people who worship "God." It seems their version of a God is a far cry from the belief of God in other parts of the world. Are we slipping back millenniums in time to more than one God again or does God serve different parts of the world differently? Who's radical, the east or the west? Who's religiously or spiritually right? Who wants peace? Who wants war? Who wants their own way? Can we all have our own way all the time?

All the intelligence developed around the world for thousands of years, technical and spiritual, certainly doesn't seem to be solving the major problems of the people and their desires to be peaceful and get along with each other.

Yes, this "is" a real important time in an era that could be depressive and destructive to mankind as a whole or an uplifting time of nourishingly new spiritual aspects that eliminates prejudices, hate and annihilative attitudes and methods.

This is a time when we of the world as a whole can utilize our bloodily and sacrificially fought for intelligence to cooperatively join one another as compared to eliminating one another through resentful, unforgiving, spiteful, narrow-minded and misleading attitudes.

Then we can extend that non-partial and flexible intelligence to collaborate with creative projects including advanced views on spirituality while utilizing past spiritual concepts as references and experiences which may be helpful and/or supportive just as books are in libraries.

Eliminating doubts, fears, misunderstanding and deceptions "can" be accomplished. Then, we can much more easily handle the population extension which is in the main culprit supplying and supporting the new and intensive problems of the twentieth and twenty first centuries. First things have always been known for having to come first and that it the most important of all.

Check this out: As the world's population grows, the outdated aspects of spiritual belief is still contentious with the threat of war and world domination. One thing grows and the next thing feeds on it and grows. The next thing appears and feeds on the last one. When does it stop? It won't take care of itself without annihilating us all! Are we that stupid? An epocal evolution? An important time to change? Yes to both. Now that we are becoming more aware of that opportunity to improve ourselves morally, spiritually and worldly for survival purposes, we can make the changes and/or additions and subtractions. We can do it in our individual way by continuing to gain more consciousness of the spiritual opportunities of our future and observing the hazardous dangers we all face with our thinking, feeling and believing.

The invisible cancer of stagnated spirituality is slowly devouring our world of supposedly good people. Trust in anything pertaining to people has signs of faltering. If we don't change our ways, none of us will any longer be fit to maintain a favorable world. A few can help, but it now requires all of us to redevelop the deteriorating world stability we brought on ourselves living in a combination of fantasy and self-centered consciousness.

The changing of the times has always been a little rough in its beginning, but glorious surprises emerged as a result of them. Now we are beginning to pass through a number of mighty changes with nations joining in attempts to maintain a nonwar world and efforts are being pursued to offset the very threatening climate change along with increasing crime etc., etc.

Flowing along with the spiritual changes is just another phase in the long-term story of planet Earth. However those changes do occur, they are bound to upgrade our states of consciousness gearing for peace among mankind when cooperation becomes the order of the day. Getting the spirit will help this epocal evolution.

Chapter 16

Preparing for mental sustenance

We are entering into a transitionary time when mankind's past and present experiences, contentions, attitudes, adaptabilities, approaches, resistances, conformities, beliefs and cooperation are to the point of being severely tested. We are faced, for those of us who allow it, with having to alter our set mannerisms because of a fastly changing world or be vacuumed in to what is becoming a keenly preprogrammed scheme of professionalized exploiters who are committed to mentally, emotionally, physically, socially and spiritually enslave everyone on planet Earth for the purpose of "feeding" specific causes of which are becoming more obvious as time passes. That's another story.

The perpetrators of the growing causes enslaving others geographically, morally and spiritually can only be offset and inevitably stopped by everyone's cooperation in broadening their spiritual scope beyond what has been established. That means escaping the state of mind known as denial. Denial is denying any other possibility. It is being insecurely norrow in mental and emotional scope and is a firmly established and set manner of mind of which is vulnerable to weakening and cracking because of inflexibility. Let us not all become victims of it.

The indicated perpetrators are not only totalitarian, hierarchal and aggressive strategists, but are now the exploited followers who are perpetuating the cause of "all" human exploitation around the globe.

This program of world domination has religious and monetary ties and support. They are engaging in stealthy progress of taking unfair advantage of the remaining pure and unsuspecting balance of the world's people. They will also become the victims.

This is not a script of a political or crusading nature, so details of specific names and places are purposely left out. The intent of these scripts is to be instrumental in raising one's consciousness awareness of impending change, probabilities, inevitabilities and opportunities for preventive and/or adaptive purposes; whatever one exercises one's birthright privilege to choose. We can view the overall and specific situations through plain glasses or rose colored glasses. It is always left to choose.

Pleasant and secure thoughts linger when all the people become aware and work on themselves for a more rewarding cause of freedom and prosperity, but how realistic is that prognostication? It is as real as all the people believe it is or can be. Odds are only against it if all the people remain naive, passively unknowledgeable and spread human expansion.

Isn't it fastenating when people hear about a romantic, social or political scandal. They can't wait to spread the story around as far as they possibly can, but when it pertains to matters of history, state affairs or religious differences, they don't seem so energetic or enthused.

Well, it also seems people need a good scare before they act. That's one reason why this era of time is so important. This is a time to reflect on what has happened with humanity's survival by resting our material progresses for awhile and put more energy into salvaging our overworked minds and rejuvenating our spiritual beliefs. It isn't just about spiritual salvation where so many people have been vacuumed into and believing over a long period of time. It's also about preventing environment contamination of our mental and emotional disposition, existence, security and capacity to say the least. That preventive approach allows us the opportunity to, like they say, open new doors and windows for reorganizing a more advanced and future oriented state of mental, emotional and spiritual stability and calmness.

The past has unveiled a ton of education and a trillion mistakes. The old times weren't much involved in preventive consciousness. It's kind of new. Now we do possess a much higher degree of it for access and useful purposes. Let's not let it idle or go to waste. Let's nourish and develop it more for the benefit of creatively expanding our spiritual consciousness, not maintaining an archaically established system of dormant philosophy that contributes to human exploitation, indoctrination and domination of the human spirit and chaotic end.

What is human domination? It is a process or taking over the mind and body by exploiting, indoctrinating and rerouting free will to trained will. Trained will is a state of mind that submits to absorbing rules and creed typical of government, religious influence and commercial dominators.

Is that what we want? Indubitably not. Freedom to be, express and participate any way we choose is one of the best life's attributes we have. It's worth keeping, protecting and preventing its seizure. We can do it in the peace and quite of our own environment.

Mental stability isn't always what one thinks it is. China passed through a period of complete mental domination whereas Americans would have resisted it all from their beginning. The people of North Korea are mentally dominated with no outside influence and have no truthful knowledge of anything outside of their country. Are they protected or are they imprisoned? China is allowed a certain amount of mental freedom and will eventually expand that freedom into a democratic society of which will release restrictions on spiritual views and beliefs that, in turn, will affect their form of government. Theoretically, the results will allow mental and spiritual freedom as in the U.S. and elsewhere.

The mental and spiritual freedom in North Korea is questionable at present. They are "stuck" in a perpetuation of discipline and routine that has no foreseeable change and developing spirituality of conventional societies is unknown to them; in particular their young people.

Most of us in free societies of the world have unlimited opportunities to develop, alter or change our mental and emotional state of mind along with our spiritual abilities, attitudes, desires and beliefs. We let them remain as is because fear of mistakes at the helm may create a worse situation in a time of change and new developments.

The spirit of mind is an inspiring and perpetual influence on and in bold action to innovate choosing another method of believing. New and less inhibited stretching of the mind allows and creates more views and alternatives. Spiritual security doesn't need stretching or developing. It's always there wherever the human mind is active, believing, promoting or observing.

Chapter 17

The work of maintaining spiritual stability

The spirit of a political convention for a presidential candidate is very "high" and everyone "feels" it. The emotional vibrations certainly do not need stimulating. The same exciting feelings occur at auto racing, horse races or when dancing vigorously. Sky diving? Bungy jumping? How about the spirited feelings one experiences with the musical sounds and beat while singing gospel songs at a lively church session? All those activities; even a job of employment can be dazzling and overpowering with emotional continuity like starring in a movie, being a foreign dignitary, working with animals, teaching dance or even pouring cement at a high rise building.

No one has to work at stimulating those mentioned activities. The people are just vibrantly engrossed in their chosen endeavors and are saturated with an enthusiasm of unpretentious and unpresumptuous spirit that exists with their spiritual motivation. That spiritual motivation is truly debatable with many views of its source. Regardless of a majority agreed answer or not, it is still there when it is there.

The preceding review and interpolation of spiritual attraction and automatic response perpetuation is not only preliminary to, but relative with efforts applied toward the materializing affects and effects of spiritual influence and its psychological and reflective support to and with a philosophy of belief that spirit exists similar to the belief of "God" existing.

Now, with the further view where spirit needs fueling and is not constantly active without it as an automobile or "anything" else requiring some source of energy behind it, we are capable and "can" initiate, perpetuate and sustain spirit of action and spirit of a belief within.

Believing of or in any kind of spirit, whether it is spirit in the self, spirit in group activity, spirit in or of God or symbol, spirit that emanates around or from a sorcerer, it all will only activate with some type of either mental or physical energy. Nothing materializes without it and everything materializes with it (materializing meaning something coming about or happening).

The power to believe and do isn't automatic or perpetuated until the power of energy is turned "on." Doing the "work" of mind development, mind stimulation, passive aggressive or even mind shrinking worthlessness, it's all needed for maintaining the power of becoming spiritually aware.

The human self is a little different than the animal self. It is stated here for purposes of understanding spiritual energy, power and individual approaches in life and any other possibilities. Animals etc., as far as we know, run, eat, sleep, fight, play and procreate from a nonevolutionary sense of habit or instinct where their inherent or received intelligence hasn't been progressively developed any more than ever. Some evolutionists believe all living beings are of the same family or protoplasmically intelligent origin. Humans are the "only" living beings capable of progressively stretching our intellect to continued new highs.

If anyone thinks and believes we would be better off reverting back to the old time ways of living, believing and existing, they may be better off reanalyzing the state and disposition we have placed ourselves in since our inception.

Once a growth of any kind of life has reached a point of advanced development, as ours has, unproductive, unhealthy, unpleasant and unhappy results of shrinkage causes irreversible deterioration which leads to the end of life similar to cutting down most trees, bushes and vines etc.

Escaping our progression of growth won't work! Utilizing efforts of innovatively probing into new and futuristically insightful methods for developing concepts to improve our consciousness along with a much overdue revision of our spiritual mannerisms, adaptations, approaches and expansion will allow new and healthy spiritual growth. Spiritual growth is simply becoming more aware of it.

History of the past in a very few years has shown readable signs where evolutionary results of conventional spirituality isn't effectively functioning as it did centuries ago or more. The developing growth periods of the past have reached their peaks the same as a tall tree, a tall old building, an ineffectively prepared business or even a marriage where they socially, intimately and intellectually grew and matured in different directions.

Everything develops, ages, changes and inevitably ends when it follows the natural course of repetition and habit. That's a pretty stark reality of which is difficult for many to accept. There are however, alternate degrees of options for those who care to adopt a theory of new growth and flexibility where spirituality, spiritual ability and spiritual awareness only needs occasional revisiting, review and reorientation.

These scripts are a part of the inevitable reformation of spiritual consciousness for broadening inhibitory restraints on self-sufficiency, self-perpetuation, self-sustainment and self-confidence.

Once the process of gaining all this wonderful and creative consciousness for more meaningful purposes in believing begins, the easier self-sustaining belief becomes and continues. It's much easier and more effective to work, pray and program to the self than to do something which is only known by what someone else says.

The stance where we are supposed to believe what someone else says, verbally or in any book, doesn't validate our adhering to it. There are too many beliefs and all of them claim they are right which, in many manners of thinking cancels them all. That deserves delving into.

Now with spiritual expectations and beliefs put on the table, adapting to eliminating wasteful fears of any restricting or demanding power over us, the road to reasonably unlimited and reliable self-spiritual power can begin to form. Once this consciousness begins, it bears a similar psychological influence as accepting Christ as one's savior. One can adapt to almost "any" form of belief and watch it take hold. That's what is so comfortably assuring about eliminating any "old" beliefs. They can be reorganized to "work" even better than ever with the self at the controls. Once one gets the drift, more understanding allows more uninhibited choices and all unnecessary fears will go down the tube the same as the sky is the limit.

Many of the readers may realize by now, in view of reading this far, the manner of believing isn't nearly as important or meaningful as having the freedom to "choose" the manner of believing. Spiritual stability is only as effective as what one can believe "after" having clear sailing options, not because of outdated expectations all based on penalties if not complied to, but because those options allows one to decipher how to better understand spiritual advantages and stability of its existence.

Spiritual stability will sustain or progress in mental, emotional, psychological, philosophical "and/or" acquired spiritual levels depending on the traditional or cultural training or other influence one has had. We exist in spiritual cognizance from a combination partly of genetical nature and partly of programmed make-up.

Without any influence of training or guidance, an individual will live day to day on sheer genetical instinct. Not good, not bad, just is.

Normal influence, of which it seems has been plenty of, creates a certain amount of study and maybe compares various methods of spirit. Encouragement from spiritual gurus tends to vacuum individuals into further study.

More interest in what spiritual aspects of life and/ or death is all about usually from more inquisitively minded individuals, involve much more study from extensive perception and perspective which is; more work allows more of that understanding of spirit. These individuals tend to lead the way in spiritual, psychological and metaphysical centers of various sorts. Work, study and patience have been their commitment to a most meaningful contribution to a most meaningful cause for comfort and stability of mind consciousness.

Chapter 18
_____

The abstract concept of spirit

A canvas painting is only abstract by virtue of how the painter sees it or by someone elses interpretation. It is "not" abstract like we all interpret concrete as hard.

Probing into various views on spirit in these chapters may present spirit or spirituality as being at least somewhat tangible and practical, but most of the time very difficult to draw a picture of unless it's like a halloween version of a ghost, a female image of divine nature. How about a scene of clouds, lightness and darkness or a peaceful retreat in a green meadow?

The absence of a picture or perceptive view could designate spirit as being more abstract than not since the essence of the term abstract appears as something either not obvious, vague, not visible, left out or can be detected when creatively imagined or believed.

The question may arise, "What is so important about a discourse on abstract concepts?" Good question. Here is reason:

Much in the area of religious, philosophical, scientific, mystical, community or moral spirit is taught more than sought. That means rules, regulations and general guidelines are focused on the subjects mentioned and not so much intricacy on the spiritual aspect of them; especially the aspect where people do not see, touch, hear, taste or even imagine yet in their maturing process. There is so much time spent on getting the general jests of those subjects, time isn't allowed to dwell and really understand the very delicately and misunderstood value of spirituality. Even the words spirit, spiritual and spirituality are thought as having different meaning; for instance in the divine spirit, the spiritual beliefs in metaphysics, the spirituality in American republicans as compared to communist Chinese or the individual right for anyone to experience their own spirituality in any manner they choose, bar none and yet all three of those words have a common denominator. They are connected to either a beginning, a maturing or a permanently established system of believing; conventional or other.

Common denominators pertaining to human perception and exchanges with one another tend to exist as a natural function in preventing all of us from focusing on one object or subject the same as all robots do.

Therefore, the complexities of abstract projections from the painter may be pure distraction of someone else attempting to understand the painter's intensions if the painter "had" intensions. Some of them don't. They just slop it on and call it abstract. Don't be a victim of inappropriate abstract "claims." Also, don't be a victim of misunderstanding what abstract concepts are or what spirit is.

An abstract of anything isn't what it is sensed to be. It is a perception of what is behind it, what motivates it and what makes it complete or to be as one meant for it to be. Shakespeare said, "To be or not to be, that is the question." More clearly stated would have been, "To be or not to be is for you to discover, so you better get with it." A much better version not involving energy to analyze or understand was introduced by the Zens of India and developed further through China and Japan originally thousands of years ago as, "What is-----is" and certainly had no criteria or impetus for understanding at least in that era of time.

Coming up to date in this era of having to understand more of everything in a time of more information than ever, we are in better positions to more substantially understand and absorb many abstract occurrences and projections in the fields of art, advertisements, politics, health, societal classes of people, monetarial employment and investment objectives, relationship complications, questionable international entanglement and even way overdue religious consciousness variations and views on spiritual transformation. They are all subject to abstract variations; some by premeditative preditors and unfair opportunists and some are only inherently natural like the spirit a person with a mediocre income may experience when winning a sizeable lottery. Some can handle it and some are led very much astray. Spirituality strays too.

Many people are led astray in the area of spirit and their own spirituality. There is a strong tendency for humans, as compared to animals and insects etc., to be attracted to any abstract sense, theory, belief or illusion where they are so important and needed; especially when they are conceived and/or ruled by a completely incomprehensive and "abstract" concept of a supernatural "being" of which many people believe is a man and they will somehow, without having a slightest clue, ascend to some other dimension after they have expired. To each his own until learned differently.

The design of life is what it "is" if you will, by some kind of inconceivable intelligence of which we obviously weren't supplied. It may not even be intelligence for all we know. Talk about abstract concepts. Anything can be anything!

Human abstractivity has its limits, at least with our comprehension for now. Let us discontinue biting off our noses to spite our faces in attempting to conjure and justify unsound beliefs of man maid fantasy where there is no provable source.

Let us adopt ways of believing where we can identify as provable to our way of thinking as humans, not subjects of speculative fantasy. We can integrate all our past and present beliefs with new concepts of spiritual consciousness that will create peace, contentment and realistic goodwill among our world of people while eliminating spiritual conflicts, insecurities and unrealistic expectations and illusions.

Yes, just like government politics, there is work to be intelligently, realistically, logically, sensibly, cooperatively and spiritually accomplished for reforming and reeducating from a whole pool of ideas which support new and "compiled" strengths of spirituality and eliminates so very much doubt socially, personally, psychologically, nationally and internationally. Let us pool our sources to learn more concerning abstracts among "all" of us and not just a few and adapt to "new" concepts of spirit and spirituality.

Abstract concepts have been notoriously known as only understood by those who possess grandeur and pompous attitudes of superior knowledge while the majority drowns in lack of brain power to understand what they mean which in many cases can be a deception for manipulating one to buy a product or service etc.

Learning abstract concepts can also "help" people understand how to prevent waste that could resolve differences between, in particular, spiritual comprehension and social contentions. There are so many opportunities to expand spiritual consciousness and relating intelligence for dealing with on planet Earth. Let us build "real" security within and be the recipients of our own spirituality which will be no threat to anyone or anything else and just possibly create that long awaited peace on Earth.

These closing words are meant to stimulate spiritual thought for whatever road one may decide to remain on or travel forward to. The content within is only a speck in the haystack of consciousness and change that will occur as time passes into the future. One can surely remain living in the past or one can choose to be a part of the endless perception of consciousness available with the unfolding future moving forward. It belongs to us all for whatever way we choose based on what we have to choose with from our learned experiences.

There is really no need to be overly concerned about an abstract understanding of spiritual existence or concept of it. The main objective in this book of spiritual consciousness is for possibly acquiring a little more cognitive awareness of spiritual possibilities one may have missed or have been looking for along the path of life because of the so very many methods of thinking, believing and feeling available. The world of spirituality is endless and constantly open for inspection. Let's exercise it. There is plenty of it.

Remember also, we can live in the "future" where freedom of thought, belief and speech is the order of the day and is not punished for blasphemy or any other narrow minded power of authority from the past or present. Get the spirit.

Your author, Lloyd E. McIlveen unveils a chronological list of many and various book subjects presenting controversial, educational, uplifting, futuristic, self-helping, philosophical, psychological, entertaining and other stimulating concepts of which are and will be displayed with brief descriptions of each book as follows:

1. "Evaluating Outdated Beliefs" This is a report, viewed through the perception of your author of the evolutionary process and changes occurring in belief; especially in the area of religion and spirituality, This was designed for the benefit of broadening individual perception, perspective and viewing "another" plane of belief while revealing fallacies in theological indoctrination. This is an improved revision of the book's origin.

2. "Staying Alive On Planet Earth I" This is a psychology of health required to stabilize and

maintain better health for the benefit of living a much longer life. Source: A lifetime of study, problems, recoveries and many successes more in natural methods.

3. "Understanding Loss To Relieve The Anguish" Loss of anything involves many distractions and disrupting emotional disarray. Gaining greater understanding of these emotions offsets the misery of them and enhances optimism of confidence and support for emotional weakness before, at and during the time of loss.

4. "Understanding Preventing And Eliminating Cancer" presents new views on the wonders of natural methods for practical use.

5. "Paradox Of Progress Unfolding I" This is a tale told by a man "many" centuries into the future about an exciting, overwhelming and terrifying occurrence on planet Earth as a result of their wondrous progress around the time of 2300

A.D. Hang onto your seats! #2 is a second issue later on the list.

6. "Offsetting Climate Change And Nuclear Waste Contamination" This view of the two exposes the hazards, inevitabilities and possible solutions needed now for preventing a "too late" disaster that will affect all living beings too soon.

7. "What God Is And Is Not" This is a study of spiritual possibilities designed, not particularly to remold conventional mannerisms of belief, but to open and expand perception in the most controversial subject of mankind; the subject of God and whether mankind will or won't expand that consciousness along with all progress and growth on Earth and in the universe.

8. "Kids Of The Crick" This is a story of four old fashioned country kids setting out on a weekend adventure in their countryside of tall

grass, mountains, rivers, animals, caves and strange living beings. Sometimes, they aren't sure whether it's all real or not.

9. "Paradox Of Destiny Explained" eliminates the mysteries, facades, fantasies and deceptions of how, where, way and when we do what we do and opens new possibilities for expanding our beliefs and consciousness pertaining to this study of available options that may influence insight for growth, change or even justify present mannerisms of what may control the individual, planet Earth or the whole universe and is not zealous, fanatic or bigoted; only assertively revealing.

10. "Paradox Of Progress Unfolding 2" This book is a continued fiction story and can be considered exemplary of "major" human changes that alienated millions of people to another planet in the future. They are led by the elements of unexpected surprises of

which is par for the course with gutsy space pioneers. The first "Paradox Of Progress Unfolding I" must be read first to understand and appreciate the disproportional attitudes and positions of people on a threshold of major change and disasters upon them. This is not only a tale of travel, trials and tribulations, it is philosophically stimulating and adds toward future insightful expansion of the human species.

11. "Staying Alive On Planet Earth 2" This is an extended version of the original psychology of health for living a longer life. More knowledge allows more life.

12. "Preventing The Doom Of Mankind" This is a stimulating, vitalizing and somewhat shocking description of how mankind is "truly" faced with extinction in the "near" future due to their own faults of progress. It's very educational and needed now to help offset that inevitability

where the odds dictate we will all perish if we don't adhere to this offsetting of which "is" possible to achieve.

13. "Spiritual Transformation Of The Fourth Millennium" Old-time conventional religion is fading. New-time spirituality is on the rise. Objective realism is the prime issue here for future inclined thinking and believing.

14. "Understanding The Science Of Creative Mind" This is a study for discovering, developing and practicing a psychological powerhouse within for conquering the unconquerable, achieving the impossible or doing things no one has done all depending on, of course, the makeup and determination of the individual. This study brings out a greater potential of the individual's abilities when taken seriously. This was compiled from a lifetime of study and experience from your author.

15. "Living to 150" is a guidance program for intentions of anyone desiring a longer than longer life which is insightfully and innovatively educational for that purpose.

16. "The Act Of Getting One's Act Together" If anyone, business or nation wants to develop their stance, priorities and position in life, this is a chance for them to get their act together more than ever.

17. "Making Changes From This Point Forward" The design of this book is for the purpose of preventing repeated mistakes of unforeseen surprises due to what we weren't or aren't aware of that did, can or will happen again. It's all about gaining or rearranging change consciousness in this area.

18. "Relationships For All" This is a carefully arranged view of how relationships can function much better when initiated or guided by the experiences of many experts and your

author who have had failures and successes in their very human encounters. The experiences of more relationships result in wiser judgments and approaches to others.

19. "The We Between Us" helps us in discovering who is good for us and who is not. First it is a study in the book. Then it is a study with people of what exists in two party's minds (individuals business or nations) when first confronted. A real time saver in evaluating possible compatibility or not between the two for anyone. It works.

20. "Passion Of Dance" This is a narrative on progress, value and guidance for the dance inclined. It's informative and inspiring with its history and recent magnetism.

21. "Open That Door" to love. This book is comprehensively all about love. It's not a storybook. It clears up the differences of love

that causes misunderstanding, suspicion and deception.

22. "Get The Spirit" This book describes controversial and somewhat intertwined conventional views of spirit, spirits and spirituality. This book untangles the "usual" views and presents a more perspective manner of living with these concepts of mind.

23. "Stories Of What They Couldn't Or Wouldn't Tell" Ages are from babies to 100 years; twenty four of them.

24. "Improving On Love And Relationships" This one is two books in one. Part one "Open That Door" is a psychology of love that enhances perspective to understand and adapt to a very popular, but deceiving, repressed and ignored emotion; love. Part two covers "Relationships For All" which elaborates on origination, different types, significance, deceptions, desires, experiences,

communication, possibilities, future and guidance of relationships. It's comprehensive and also derived from a lifetime of relationship experiences and serious study.

NOTES

NOTES

NOTES

NOTES

NOTES

www.ingramcontent.com/pod-product-compliance
Lightning Source LLC
Chambersburg PA
CBHW030440290526
45786CB00001B/373